The Messy Truth About Leading People

It Ain't Easy!

Nicki Roth and Gavin Fenn-Smith

ISBN 9798637875641
Imprint: Independently published

Any references to historical events, real people, or real places are used
fictitiously. Names, characters, and places are products of the authors'
imaginations.

Illustrations by Anjora Noronha

Printed in the United States of America.

www.themessytruthleadership.com

We are indebted to all the leaders we've encountered over the years. We have seen them be brave, stupid, arrogant, wise, nuanced, humble, driven, kind and a million other traits. Collectively, they have helped us understand that leading is hard, complicated and filled with twists and turns. We applaud their humanity and courage.

To those reading this, we wish you great success. We urge you to keep your sense of humor. You're going to need it!

MICAH'S TWISTY-TURNY JOURNEY

The Messy Truth
About Leading People

INTRODUCTION

For decades, we have been passionate students and practitioners of leadership and organizational change. We relied on scholarly research, bright colleagues and thought leaders to inform our work. This wisdom was invaluable. But not enough.

As consultants and leaders, we kept bumping up against the gap between well-founded theories and the reality on the ground for leaders. Applying established methodologies did not always lead to the expected outcomes. It turns out that leadership is much messier than those books on the shelves led us to believe.

It became obvious to us that a deep understanding of human beings was missing from the conversation.

We humans are not widgets and we often respond in surprising ways. We emote, even when we are quiet and reserved. We compete with our peers and crave approval from our boss. We attempt to be good team players but frequently fall short. Our egos bring out the best and the worst in us. We search for our compadres, even if they are a bad influence. We play politics hoping to triumph over others. We harbor hidden agendas and strong desires to please. We are often unconscious of the negative or positive impact we have on the people around us. In short, we humans are complicated.

Organizations are a collection of people sitting inside of formal and informal hierarchies and cultures. That is a very jumbled stew yet few among us are well prepared to handle all these dynamics. Leadership training may provide some useful information, but not enough.

Great leaders connect with, and tap into, the richness and complexity of their people. They perceive the interaction patterns in their teams and have the insight and courage to steer them successfully. They are self-reflective and honest about their strengths and shortcomings. And they are invested in growth; their own and others.

Imagine seeing, hearing, reading all the thought bubbles that constantly float above real leaders' heads. The thoughts that are rarely shared, usually censored, but are the raw truth about leading people. And then consider learning solutions to some of the most infuriating frustrations or as we call them, Stupid Human Tricks. That's what this book is about.

The characters you are about to meet are based on true stories. They will feel familiar to you. They are imperfect with great strengths and painful flaws. Some learn from their mistakes while others don't. Some succeed and others flame out. But all are perfectly, remarkably, ridiculously human.

MEET MICAH

I'll spare you the trouble of turning to the last page and tell you how it ends. I do become a successful CEO, I no longer believe in the myth of work-life balance, and I still have a soul. If you had asked me 20 years ago if any of this was possible, I would have bullshitted you and said, "Of course!" What I would have kept to myself was, "I have big ambitions and not the slightest idea what the fuck I'm doing."

This describes a typical day early in my career. I'd wake up stressed, drink loads of coffee, tap out shit on my computer while getting ready to leave my apartment, get to the office early hoping to arrive before my boss (rarely happened), spend the day in meetings competing to sound like the smartest one in the room, stay late to respond to emails that flooded my inbox while sitting in all those crappy meetings, try to leave after my boss (rarely happened) and get home with some carryout food and flop down on the couch before working some more before sleep. Next day: rinse, repeat. I questioned the insanity of this endless cycle frequently. Is this what paying my dues meant? Did the long-and-not-always-meaningful hours equate with learning or value or was it all just bullshit? Was I in training to become "The Man" and was that what I wanted? Did I like the person I was becoming? I was always the square peg trying to fit into the round hole; was this job rounding out my beloved edges and turning me into a clone? Was I disappearing myself?

Despite this nagging inner dialogue, I drudged onward and upward with so many ups and downs along the way. That's the thing they don't tell you in B-school. Where's the chapter on "Your career will be fraught with more doubts than certainties and more anxieties than you want to imagine, so get used to it"? If I had known this at the start, would I have made different choices? Would I have written the great American novel or become a professional skier or a master teacher or the head of a charitable foundation instead? Like any of those choices would prevent me from having to slog through mounds of second-guessing and wondering if I made terrible life choices. Most days I was full steam ahead, making the best of my chosen profession.

By mid-career I added something new to my morning rituals. I call it my "All That Jazz" wake up call. Remember that scene in the movie about Bob Fosse where he stumbles into the bathroom each morning, splashes his face with cold water, squeezes eye drops into each bloodshot eye and stares at his reflection in the mirror? He fakes a smile, snaps his fingers and pronounces "Showtime!" and heads out the door. "Showtime" was my morning mantra as I increasingly felt like I was more performance art than that lovely square-pegged true self.

On a less conscious level (which is where I resided most of the time), I was getting more relaxed and willing to behave more like myself and less like a robot. That meant not always following the rules, speaking more truthfully, doing more of what I thought mattered, prioritizing human stuff over mathematical measures, challenging the status quo, and believing that I could be the leader I wanted to be. The template I was supposed to follow just didn't fit. For that matter, it didn't thrill most of the people I worked with. Not for the first time in my life, I just said, "Fuck it. I'm going to do me."

And as you read in the first sentence, that turned out just fine. As I sit here in my office and look out at, well, the parking lot, it is easy for me to remember the bright and dark moments along the way. I met people who taught me what I did and did not want to be. I tried things I felt competent at and more things that scared me. I succeeded, made mistakes (some whoppers!), and tried to fade into the wood-work at times. I stayed at some jobs too long and left others prematurely. I worried too much about the wrong stuff and not enough about the right stuff. I offended people, didn't speak up when I should have, and got it right most of the time. I took bold steps, stuck my neck out, and buried my head in the sand. In short, I was not the one-dimensional cutout I was encouraged to be. I was a complicated human being.

Again, I will spare you the trouble of reading this whole book. I'll give away the secret right here. *Leaders lead people*; not strategies or initiatives. That requires a pant-load of self-awareness and under-standing of what makes human beings tick.

And just in case you want to know more about this, you can still read the book. It may fill in the gaps from grad school or that fantastic professional library you've accumulated since then.

SHANTE, THE WISE

I entered graduate school with my ideals intact. I believed that leadership was a noble calling and had the potential to bring out the best in people and organizations. How quaint! By the time I entered the workforce, my views had become less "sunshine and daisies" and more "dungeons and dragons". Despite this new perspective, I remained hopeful that I could live up to my original naïve fantasies.

After two years in my first serious job, my optimism faded. I still liked the company I was working for but felt out of step in some fundamental ways. My peers were grinding out long hours and then hitting the bar to talk shit about our bosses. I didn't object to the long hours or alcohol. I just didn't trust these people enough to air my own grievances. I was also uncomfortable with the way my boss favored competition on the team over collaboration. I felt like a jerk every time I played well with others only to have the football pulled away at the last second. I looked around for leaders to emulate but found few I admired. Did I need to jump ship or hang in there a bit longer?

Eventually, the company offered me a "development opportunity" as part of a trendy new corporate initiative and they assigned me a mentor. "Development opportunity" meant that senior leaders were required to mentor younger staff or lose some of their year-end bonus dollars. So, whose development are we talking about? Needless to say, I was skeptical.

Shante was a senior executive I knew only by reputation. When we met for the first time, I wasn't sure how to behave. Was I supposed to impress Shante or kiss their ass? I was completely disarmed when Shante began the discussion with, "I'm here to help you succeed. Whether that is at this company or the next, I want to help you become the best leader you know how to be." Was that music coming from the parting heavens? I censored everything that was running through my brain and stayed quiet. I knew better than to trust this kind of blank check. They could make or break my career.

"I really am committed to becoming a great leader. I look forward to you unlocking the mystery of how to succeed here," I finally blurted out, opting for one part sincerity and one part flattery.

"I'm not sure you understand," continued Shante. "I don't have a magic formula with ten easy steps. Leadership is about knowing yourself, gaining support and respect from others and infusing what you do with purpose and meaning. How could I tell you what to do if, at the core of it, your capacity as a leader is about *you* being clear about who you are?"

I wondered if something snarky would work with Shante. Too soon, I decided. "Okay. Does that mean we are going to talk about me? Like therapy? I'd much rather hear about you. You are already successful. You must have so much to share with me." Too much kiss-ass?

Shante allowed a long pause to hang in the air. I was certain I had blown it in the first two minutes. You fucking idiot! Just when I thought I'd explode, Shante leaned forward.

"Micah, let me tell you a story. When I was 29 years old, I was certain I had all the answers. I had been to the best schools, got recruited by the best companies, got promoted early and often and was poised to do great things. My bosses loved me, my reviews were glowing and I was leap-frogging over my peers. It was so obvious to me that I had, in fact, unlocked the mysteries of leadership and success. I was living proof, after all.

"While I was paying such close attention to all these symbols of my achievements, my colleagues and direct reports perceived something quite different. I snapped at them, bragged about my success, didn't engage much with others and generally set myself apart and above everyone. I was so good at managing up, though, that my boss had no idea there was trouble in paradise. But there was one SVP, Avery, who saw through the smokescreen. They invited me out for lunch. Naturally, I saw this as a positive sign.

"I couldn't have been more wrong. In a very direct but supportive way, Avery told me that I was in danger of blowing up my career. They described my inflated sense of self, disrespect for my colleagues, brown-nosing the bosses and general crappiness. Despite my accomplishments, feedback was bound to get back to my boss, and I might get canned. I got defensive and pushed back but they stopped me cold and said, 'This right here. This is what I'm talking about.'

"I was stunned. Avery was someone I respected who had significant weight around the place. I had to take this seriously. I asked, 'Is there any way I can change your mind?' Their response was, 'It's not about changing my mind. It's about changing your behavior. And that will depend entirely on what you do next.' The long discussion we had next was unexpected and profound."

I was rapt. "What did Avery tell you? What did you do? What happened?"

"The short version is that, despite great guidance, I just didn't get my act together. I was fired four months after that lunch. Best thing that ever happened to me." Shante sat back and watched the seven different expressions that passed over my face. "Failure is the best teacher. I shudder to think who I would have turned out to be without that early lesson."

Wait a second! Was Shante telling me that I needed to fuck up so I could get fired to become a great leader? I was just getting out of debt. I couldn't afford to get fired. I settled into a skeptical scowl and folded my arms across my chest. This is bullshit.

Shante continued. "My point is that I wasn't able to take the best advice anyone ever gave me. A combination of my own arrogance and my inability to make any significant change caused me to flame out. Trust me, I was geared up to repeat the same mistakes at the next company. I knew that Avery had sent up the red flair but I told myself that others were just jealous of my success. The best gift I ever got was a follow up lunch with Avery after I was fired. They wouldn't let me get away without absorbing the truth. It was a tough love moment. I committed to self-reflection and a new attitude before I started my next job. Things have been different ever since."

"So, is the moral of the story your mentor is always right?" I asked.

"No. The moral of the story is not to buy your own hype. Learn to be truthful with yourself and you just might become a great leader."

This was the first of many intense, infuriating, rich, confusing, and uncomfortable conversations we had. I continued to press Shante to share pearls of wisdom that I could imprint onto my own being and Shante redirected me inward to discover my own insights. By the end of the six-month program, I wasn't sure what to make of the whole experience. On the one hand, I was more observant about my actions but on the other, I hated being self-conscious. I was used to relying on my wits with little forethought or reflection. I prided myself on not having a censoring button. It meant that I was always telling the truth. Didn't that fall in the category of "authentic leadership"?

At the close of our last meeting, Shante handed me a note with the instructions to read it later at a quiet moment. I thanked Shante for their time and help and forgot about the note until I was rummaging through my backpack later that evening. I opened the envelope and read the following:

"Leadership is the manifestation of your humanity; your connection to those who choose to join you. Don't let an organization or popular thinking pressure you to lose your compassion, your moral compass or your core self. If you do, it will end badly."

Well, that's rather ominous, I thought. Over the months, Shante had hammered away at my people issues. This was quite a departure from what my boss was asking me to do. In fact, the demands of my job could be achieved so much more easily if I didn't have to deal with those idiots on my team. The devil on one shoulder was push-ing me in a heartless direction while the Shante angel was telling me to look behind door number two. I suck at making these kinds of decisions.

I shoved Shante's note back into my backpack and relieved the brain pain with a cold beer.

THE GAME AND ITS PLAYERS

Despite the meaningful conversations with Shante, I struggled to reconcile their guidance with the reality I faced. My boss laid more responsibility at my feet and expressed confidence in my abilities to surpass all expectations. My life outside of work had already dwindled to only showing up for holidays and weddings. I justified this extreme imbalance by telling myself to bang it out now while I was still young. Occasional texts with friends-I-used-to-hang-with passed for deep personal connections. I riveted my energy on my team and results.

I did apply one piece of Shante's advice; watch others to find both positive and negative role models. This evolved into a deeply ingrained habit that I still use today. I call it: Do This-Don't Do That. Some people collect shoes or ball caps, I collect characters.

Lee was a Senior Director that I interacted with frequently. They were straight forward, competent and not afraid to question the status quo. In meetings, I noticed how Lee asked questions to draw out others and used "we" far more than "I". They had a way of lighting up the conversation, motivating everyone. It could be over the top, but Lee had a knack for getting everyone involved to agree on a plan and get shit done. Everyone's ideas were "great" or "interesting" and it seemed that no one felt like an idiot when Lee was running the meeting. I knew that Lee had been in the military and I wondered if this team approach was a holdover from that training. Lee was on my "Do This" side of the leadership ledger.

When I first met Jay, I wasn't sure what to make of them. Self-confident, smart, and ambitious. They used a lot of the preferred company language: development, quality, results, solutions, authenticity. Blah, blah, blah. The senior people took a shine to Jay and they were tapped for impressive assignments and recognition. The more I observed Jay, the more I mistrusted them. They had a way of uncovering other people's vulnerabilities without revealing a thing about themselves. While Jay remained opaque, they used others' sore spots to set them off balance. While someone wobbled, Jay swooped in to save the day, take the floor or smugly sidle up to the most senior person in the room. I came to realize that Jay was a whole ball of insecurities with some malintent and someone to be avoided. Definitely, on the "Don't Do That" list. Worse than my displeasure with Jay was my nausea with their organizational ascent. They were a master at playing The Game and to that victor went the spoils. I committed myself to playing The Game on my own terms. The thought of needing to turn into Jay revolted me. But at this point, I had no fucking clue what my terms would look like.

To Lee and Jay's extremes, I noticed Tony's middle-of-the-road behavior. In groups, they were a wallflower and only spoke up when their expertise was needed. One-on-one, Tony was a spitfire. Smart, concise, helpful, engaging. I loved seeking their advice. One day, after we had taken care of business, I asked Tony why they were so passive in meetings and so active alone. They said, "Those large meetings are for show horses. All braying and prancing and no substance. I'm a work horse and prefer settings where I can get shit done." The only problem with this approach was that the executives never felt Tony had serious leadership chops and would never promote them beyond the Director level. Tony didn't make it onto either of my lists because I had too many questions. Did I have to be a show horse to be seen as a leader? Would I limit my career if I didn't appear to value these group dynamics by playing along? Didn't the other people in the room know how silly these conversations were?

But a nagging question always seemed to resurface as I watched my fellow travelers: If I don't like the rules of The Game, can I change it and stay employed? At this point in my career, I noticed many people who played The Game were assholes and not who I wanted to become. Conversely, many admirable people were languishing on the vine because they "didn't have fire in the belly". Fire in the belly sounds like heartburn or ulcers to me; a painful condition that leads to poor health. Ever the optimist, I charged forward believing that I didn't have to self-immolate to succeed.

TRYING TO PLAY WELL
WITH OTHERS

During those years, I also struggled with various group dynamics. I was on three teams: a departmental team with my peers, a cross-functional team, and a project team. As a member, I was expected to proactively speak up, provide input into decision making, complete tasks to support the team's work and to generally be collaborative. I began to conclude that teams are great in theory but suck in reality.

I tried to be a good teammate. I showed up prepared, I finished assignments on time, I listened to others and supported their efforts. I was positive in my outlook. As a reward, I received a few pats on the back from my boss and a whole bunch of crap from my colleagues. They resented my eager-beaver routine and claimed that it made it difficult for them to say that the objectives were too aggressive. If only I could lower my performance standards, then the team could unify around its mediocrity. Of course, they didn't say it in those words. Instead, I got a steady stream of "Look who's kissing up today," and "Who died and made you the boss?" And to complete the lunacy, the least qualified people seemed to take control of every conversation.

You can imagine the mind fuck this was for me. So, if I uphold the contract of being a good team player I'm actually being a bad team player? I was supposed to play to a lower common denominator to be one of the gang? Why couldn't it work in reverse? Why couldn't they all up their games to meet my high standards so we could kill it together? None of this made sense to me. I culled my memory banks to see if something in my past would enlighten me. The sports teams I was on were all motivated to win. If you didn't show up and work hard you were kicked off. Dragging the team down was not an option. I was on committees that were lackluster but I didn't get the evil eye for being engaged and gung-ho. What was it about a company setting that made my experiences on teams so shitty?

This was so aggravating that I set up a time to talk with Shante about this after our formal mentoring had ended. I plopped down in their office and resisted the urge to launch into a ten minute rant. Instead I asked, "Remind me again what you told me about teams."

Was that a smirk before they spoke? "When I reflect on what I have learned about teams, I am reminded of that fairy tale about the princess and the frog. I had to kiss a lot of frogs before I found a prince!"

"Oh, great! Lots of disappointment before I encounter a decent team. Just what I was hoping to hear."

Shante continued. "When we interact one-on-one, most of us do just fine. As you keep adding people to the conversation, it gets more layered and complicated. You have to pay attention to ten people's emotions, expressed ideas, non-verbal cues, unexpressed stuff and motivations. Then you have to notice who is speaking a lot or not at all. You have to track whether or not anything is getting accomplished or if things have gone completely off the rails. Herding cats comes to mind. Frogs, cats. Groups tend to bring out our more primal behaviors: following the leader, conformity, survival, lashing out when attacked, avoiding danger. In humans that translates to someone who is dominant keeping everyone in line and trying to minimize bad outcomes. When you stand out from the pack, that can be felt as a threatening situation.

"Of course, this is all contrary to what the company *says* it wants from teams. We leaders instruct you to question the status quo, offer new ideas, push for excellence, engage in productive debates, include all members in the discussion and consider contrarian views. That is what we say but we are aware that few teams actually achieve that."

Still confused, I asked, "So, what am I supposed to do? If I act like a responsible team player and do what my boss wants, my team hates me and we suck at getting the job done. If I join the pack, I'll hate myself. I will be acting in ways that aren't who I am and I will be part of a losing effort. No thanks!"

"Micah, let me ask you a question. What is more important to you? Fitting in or being true to yourself?"

The light bulb went off in my head. "Oh, that was very clever, Shante, bringing me full circle like that. All those months of you pushing me to dig deep inside myself to get clear about who I am and who I want to be. And me always looking outside myself to figure out how to fit in. I just got it! I need to know myself and succeed on my own terms otherwise things will go sideways. I may be slow but I finally get your point."

"Hey, the good news is that you may save yourself from being fired like I was! This is a huge lesson, Micah. Let me say this to you one more time. Those moments of frustration when you feel out of step? That is your core self signaling to you, 'pay attention, danger ahead'. It is your system's way of saying something is wrong here and it is important to discern if it is you or your surroundings. Sometimes it *will* be you. You will have done something that is outside your personal moral code and you need to clean things up. More frequently it will be someone or something that just doesn't work for you. That problem solving can be more difficult."

Holy shit. I asked Shante to hold on for a second while I wrote myself a note. "Celebrate your square peg-ness. Resist joining a gang. You don't want to be imprisoned."

But that still left me with the problem of how to operate in teams that sucked. I asked Shante again, "Okay, if I stay true to myself, how can I function on a team? By definition, a team requires everyone to join in."

"That's true but you don't have to play by others' rules. Continue to play by your standards. A few things will happen. One, you will feel good about yourself. Two, others will either keep being jerks or they will come over to your way of thinking. Three, the team will either succeed or not. Four, word will get around that you are a great team player. Five, you will get selected to be on better teams. And someday, when you are leading a team, you will have all this practice to reference."

I left Shante's office feeling both lighter and weighed down by the dread of returning to my team meetings. I had already developed awful sentiments towards some of my peers. Could I set that aside or would I rip them a new one? How would I manage the self-righteous indignation I felt? I was already thinking how much better I was than them. Would this overtake my actions? Would I just take control of the teams and go all autocratic?

That night as I ate dinner and downed a good glass of wine, I re-read the note I had written in Shante's office. If I was going to stay out of jail, I needed to find other square pegs at work. I was convinced they existed. I wondered which Affinity Group I needed to infiltrate.

MOVING ON

I stayed at this company for four years. Some days I dragged my ass into the office thinking "I can't take it anymore!" Most days I had more pragmatic thoughts. I had finally paid off my student loans, I was exposed to interesting people and projects, I was learning how to survive in a company and I had attended many global conferences in our sector. I think of those years as boot camp; lots of repetitive drills building up stamina and muscles. Too many weekly meetings, quarterly offsites, engagement surveys, new strategies, transformation agendas and restructuring that felt more like treading water than moving forward.

With each year, I became more convinced that I was going to be an awesome leader. There was no way I was going to do half of this stupid shit. I spent time picturing myself at the helm doing the most inventive and remarkable things. I was in training to understand all the things not to do as a leader. So, when a recruiter called to see if I'd jump ship to take on a more senior role at a different company, I didn't hesitate.

I arranged one last meeting with Shante before I left. I wanted to say thank you. After I heaped on the praise about their wisdom and all I had learned, Shante asked me, "What did you learn about yourself, Micah?" As I launched into my observations about how soulless corporations are, Shante stopped me.

"I didn't ask you what is wrong with corporations. I asked you what did you learn about yourself?"

I had to smile. Shante never let up. "This may surprise you, but I've been thinking about that. I even wrote some notes to myself. I came up with four insights. For one, there is a huge gravitational pull in organizations to conform and drink the Kool Aid. I never realized how much culture can shape your behavior. I haven't figured out how to find the right balance between being a good citizen and not partic- ipating in unproductive bullshit. Secondly, trusting others is tough. There is so much internal competition that pits us against each other despite calls for cooperation and inclusion. I'm not naturally inclined to back-stab to get ahead of my peers, yet the system seems to re- ward that behavior. This has caused me to be self-protective. Fortu- nately, I've found some good compadres along the way so I haven't been completely shut down. Third, this team thing is still a work in progress. I'm convinced that it is possible to be on a great team but the closest I got to that was a decent one. And lastly, which you would say is the most important, I've learned that it is hard to hold onto my sense of self. I feel like I have to leave two-thirds of myself at home. Too many ideas or emotions or questions or ambitions or jokes are not welcome. I want to believe that any company wants all I have to offer. But these years have made me question that. I have a feeling this is the core dilemma I will face wherever I work."

Shante nodded thoughtfully during my monologue. I was relieved to be more open and honest than I had been throughout our relation- ship. As I said, corporations are not the most trusting places. Since I was moving on, Shante no longer had power over me so I let it rip.

"Ah, Grasshopper, my work here is done. You have learned well," said Shante.

"What is it with you and animals? Done? What's done?"

"My guidance to you is done but your work with yourself is just get- ting started. Remember what I said during our first session? I said that leadership is about knowing yourself and what you stand for. That is a lifelong journey but you've made a very good start. Keep paying attention to your reactions and thoughts. Keep trying to bring your whole self to work. Keep trying new ways of showing up even if it goes against the norm...especially if it goes against the norm. In time, the pieces will start to fall into place and make more sense than they do today. You are well on your way to being a great leader."

With that pronouncement, I felt like I got two gold stars on my forehead and an A+ on the exam. I went back to my cubicle and packed up all the coffee cups and offsite trinkets. I still hadn't fully furnished my apartment and thought they might come in handy.

PAY ATTENTION!

There is nothing like being poached from your company when you aren't even looking for a job to make you feel like you are all-that. When the recruiter discussed the Director role at this premier corporation, I only had a few questions. Would I have direct reports and real authority to run something? Would I get a significant bump in salary and more vacation days? What was the culture like? And was there free food? Here's the thing: recruiters are salespeople who get paid to fill positions, not to tell the truth. I was naïve and wildly flattered by the title, prestige, and money. My ego was in overdrive while my good sense took a vacation.

During the interview process, there were warning signs that I ignored. My future peers were tightly wound and gave short, terse answers to my questions about what it was like to work there. I remember thinking, "Hmmm, aren't they succinct!" The two interviews with my future boss were weird. While doing everything to dissuade me from taking the job, Kelly smiled incessantly. Negative and positive simultaneously. I wondered about this schizophrenic behavior. My gut was shouting at my head to pay attention but my ego had taken control. If any doubts crept in, I told myself that I was hot shit and could deal with anything; I had superpowers. Or so I thought.

On my first day during HR orientation, the Human Resources person pulled me aside to express their relief. "Thank god someone finally accepted this position. It's been open for over a year because Kelly's

reputation scares everyone away. You must be a strong, brave soul."
I turned white and had trouble breathing. Before a serious anxiety
attack hit, I excused myself and raced to the restroom. Staring at
myself in the mirror, I shook my head. "You fucking idiot. That's another fine mess you've gotten me into! It seems you're going to need
actual superpowers to make this work."

SAKU, THE MAGICIAN

I promise I'll tell you all about Kelly. It's a long and painful story but I'd rather let you know about my team first because it was an interesting mixed bag.

Despite the shitty tone and culture Kelly had set for the department, I was committed to making my team productive and high performing. I met one-on-one with each member before starting our regular team meetings, to get to know each person and to connect with them. I made some initial assessments of each player and the implications for the group.

This was less of a team and more of a loose confederation of people who interacted only when necessary. Rather than dread, I was excited by the challenge. I was Micah, red cape and all, to the rescue. I felt I knew enough about teams at this point that I would get this right.

At our first team meeting I did everything by the book. I described our goals and objectives, shared some things about myself to let them know I was a real person, asked each person for input on how they hoped the team would operate together and made it clear they could come to me without fear of retribution. They were wary, but that was to be expected. They were mostly silent, but it was just the first meeting. The two Alphas made it clear who was boss; not me. The two

Good Soldiers smiled and nodded a lot, but fidgeted the whole time. The Underperformer and the Resistor sat back with folded arms, putting out their Do Not Disturb signs. My expectations were low but I realized I had underestimated how many superpowers I would need.

I wore myself ragged during those first six months trying to form relationships with each of my direct reports in hopes that this would accelerate our growth as a team. Check-in conversations, casual lunches, mixing up our meeting agendas, uncovering what each person needed to succeed, doling out praise and recognition, trying to get the Alphas to make space for the others, coaching the Underperformer to do better. In spite of all my efforts, after all those months, this team didn't look or sound any different than they did on my first day. What the fuck?

In a state of desperation, I talked with my HR person. I wondered if there were any training or resources available for team development. They told me that my team had already been trained. Okay. Were there any teams around the company that had a great reputation? They suggested I talk with Saku. Everyone wanted to be in Saku's group because their team loved working together.

I met with Saku to find out their secret. They suggested that I sit in on one of their team meetings and we could talk afterwards. I made myself inconspicuous in the corner and watched with amazement. Everyone spoke up in constructive ways, people really heard each other, "we" was the pronoun of choice and Saku hardly spoke at all. These folks had been together for more than two years but my team had been together longer. So, longevity did not account for the fluidity and cooperation. They also laughed and seemed to enjoy the discussion. There was lively energy with sparks flying. My team felt more like cement.

I asked Saku how they were able to create such magic. "Trust me. There was no magic here. In fact, this easily could have gone all wrong.

"Management put me in this role as the last hope for turning this part of the business around. If I couldn't spin gold in short order, this department would shut down and most of us would lose our jobs. I analyzed the business and determined that we could pull this off. I never let the team know the gravity of the situation. I didn't want anyone to think we were losers or to only be motivated to save our jobs. I just approached the team with confidence that we would succeed and they never questioned that.

"I told the team we needed to be as inventive and unorthodox as possible so our meetings were filled with forward thinking fresh ideas. We spent some time monitoring and reporting but mostly our face time together was geared towards exploring new approaches. As you saw, we openly debate alternatives and support experimenting and assess how things worked out. They work in dyads and small groups outside our formal meetings too."

If I hadn't seen it, I would never have believed it.

Saku continued, "There are a couple things I always do when joining a new team. Early on, I take everyone offsite for a couple of days for a mix of socializing and working. I believe that members need to bond with each other to work effectively as a team. My leadership of the team is less important than their collective efforts. I make it clear to the team that we are in this together and that my role is to facilitate their work rather than to drive everything. I expect them to step up and take responsibility for achieving our goals and that I am not a babysitter. I manage from the sidelines rather than on the field."

We were interrupted three times during our discussion by staff asking follow-up questions from the meeting. I noticed how relaxed Saku was and how much they sincerely trusted the team to get it done. I asked, "How is the business doing?"

"By month 10, we were nearly out of the red. By month 16, we were turning a profit and by month 20 we had developed two new lines of business to expand our reach. No one lost their job and six new people have joined the group."

Meeting with Saku energized me and inspired me to try some new things with my team. The first thing I did was fold up that red cape and tuck it away in the drawer with my XL ego. Being a successful team had nothing to do with my superpowers. The second thing I did was schedule and plan a two day offsite.

Just to be clear, I was a huge skeptic when it came to these team offsites. After attending five or six offsite meetings in the past, I recognized a pattern. I would walk into these meetings with tentative excitement and walk out with new hope. Then, a week later, I found myself wondering why we wasted the time and money. I didn't understand why the company would make these investments if there was no tangible impact. I promised myself that something would happen at the retreat that would carry over into the office. I would use all those disappointing experiences to plan a better meeting.

I invited my HR person to help with some of the planning and to facilitate the meeting so I could fully participate. The agenda wove in and out of some personal sharing and work projects. We designed the agenda with structure, but also the flexibility to adapt to unexpected developments throughout the day. It was a progressive build over the two days to get people to be more open so we could establish some trust.

The opening exercise on the second morning was meant to help the team get to know each other. It was still a low risk, safe activity that was supposed to last about 30 minutes. What happened was unexpected and pivotal. Everyone shared four pieces of information about themselves; where we grew up, the story behind our names, how many siblings we had, and one childhood challenge that had a long-term impact.

Carroll, one of the Alphas, began. "I grew up in Chicago; great city, best pizza. I was named Carroll because they were my mother's favorite cousin. I'm the oldest of four kids and my biggest challenge was how bored I was in school. The teachers finally figured out how smart I was and I ended up skipping second and fifth grades. I've always been younger than my peers but much more advanced. I got bullied a lot but my parents helped me understand that other kids were just jealous of me. It's been hard for me to fit in."

Everything about Carroll made more sense to me and I wasn't buying their self-serving bullshit. I was pretty sure no one else was either.

Next came Adrian, one of the Good Soldiers. "I grew up in a small town outside of Charlotte. Most people never went to college and never left home. It was the kind of place where everyone knows your business, both good and bad. I was named Adrian because I had a sibling named Adrian who died two years before I was born. I was the replacement third child for the one that died." With that, Adrian choked up and the rest of the team was stunned silent. The facilitator stepped in and said, "That must have been so difficult."

Suddenly, Ryan (the other Alpha) spoke up. "I had a sibling that died too. I was 14 when it happened. He was my older brother, the golden child. He was hit by a drunk driver. It crushed my parents. My mother retreated to her bedroom and my father avoided coming home. I tried to take over being the golden child as well as the parent to my other siblings. When I got a scholarship to college, I couldn't leave fast enough. I couldn't take the burden."

A floodgate had opened. We spent the next two hours sharing deeply personal and vulnerable stories. I participated and shared stuff I never would have in a work setting, especially as the boss. Everyone finally started seeing each other as human beings.

We scuttled the agenda and the group discussed how they wanted to use the rest of the day. They decided on a question and answer forum that alternated between work and personal issues. Ryan asked Adrian how they handled the whole town knowing the family business. Addison asked Carroll if they were able to make any friends along the way. Carroll asked Dion what they loved about the job. Dion asked me what I found frustrating about the company. Ryan asked Addison how they could help with the work. By the end of the day, everyone knew so much more and I sensed bonds forming. I kept my expectations in check and didn't assume anything would be different back at the office.

But it was. Not a ton, but things had shifted. The conversations had more energy, more curiosity, less tension, and better output. Collaboration improved and individual performance evened out. Staff sought me out more and trust improved. It wasn't a 10 but I was happy with this new 6.

A random-spontaneous-nothing-you-can-plan-for event catalyzed our team's transformation. This taught me that, in the end, we are all human beings. That can lead to shit shows or shape shifting moments. My central priority as team leader was to create the conditions to minimize the crap and open the door for serendipitous moments. At this point, I hadn't quite figured out how to do the latter.

WELCOME TO THE
DARK SIDE

Kelly's reputation was well-earned; they were a total nightmare. They were all the bad boss stories rolled into one: took credit for others' ideas and accomplishments, sucked up to the CEO, bad-mouthed peers, smiled to your face while putting the dagger in your back, abused direct reports in public, chewed through assistants like a woodchuck and was generally evil incarnate. I figured out quickly that I couldn't trust Kelly so I needed to figure out how to be productive and advance my own career while avoiding my boss as much as possible, which seemed at the time like an insurmountable hurdle. That would require a superpower I did not possess.

Two incidents from that first year illustrate the challenges of working with Kelly and how I tried to navigate that relationship.

I was in charge of a major project that Kelly was especially invested in and they made it clear that I better not screw this up. I asked my direct report, Adrian, to work side by side with me. Adrian was a good team player, reliable, meticulous and (most importantly) wouldn't steal any thunder from Kelly. After one of our check-in meetings, Kelly dismissed Adrian so they could speak with me privately.

"Micah, I have no idea why you thought Adrian was the right person for this assignment. What were you thinking?"

I knew I needed to be very careful about what I said. At first, I deflected the question. "I have a lot of confidence in Adrian but obviously, you have some concerns. Why don't you tell me what they are?" Avoidance, the first stage.

"Look, I'm sure that Adrian does fine with regular work but I just don't see them as having the smarts to deal with something this visible. I can't imagine them presenting to the executive team. They aren't strong enough to sell the concept." I saw where this was going so I tried stage two, sucking up.

"Kelly, trust me, I considered that. Since I always assumed that you would make the presentation, I looked for the person who would dot every 'I' so you could sell it without a worry."

"Well, since this project is so important, it does make sense that I give the talk. I'll have to figure out how to position that with the CEO. You know how they prefer that we put our teams in front of the execs instead of hogging the show."

I could see the wheels turning as I moved to stage three, the Micah finesse. "Here is how I thought we could handle that. Adrian really is the best person to pull all this together, with my oversight, of course. We will continue to meet with you until you are comfortable with the slides. At the executive meeting, I will be the team member with you. I've already let Adrian know not to expect to be there. I thought I would do an introduction, talk about the work leading up to this point, give Adrian credit in the room and then turn it over to you to walk through the specifics." I felt a little smug pulling off these Jedi mind tricks; while still supporting my team member, I prevented Kelly from ripping Adrian to shreds, still put myself in front of the execs to have some visibility, and I made Kelly feel properly kowtowed to without losing my soul.

But Kelly couldn't resist having the last word. "Sounds like a solid plan. But to be clear, I think Adrian is an idiot. You better monitor the work very closely." I held my tongue and walked out of Kelly's office. All I could think was, "What a fucking asshole. Was that necessary?"

Things only got worse. Like heart-stopping, shivers-down-the-spine worse. There was an opening for a new VP on Kelly's peer team. Several candidates interviewed with the members of that team and two people emerged as ideal candidates for the position. For some reason, Kelly wanted to chat with me about this process and the people they met. Kelly spewed vitriol about each of their peers; one was dumb, one slept around, another was only hired because of affirmative action, and no one knew the business like Kelly did. In fact, the whole company was filled with lowlife imbeciles and Kelly was the only one fit to run the show. When it came to the two finalists for the VP role, Kelly was the only one who favored candidate A over B. There was a lot of back and forth amongst the group and when it became clear that Kelly was going to lose this fight they approached the EVP in charge of the recruitment process.

Kelly kept spewing. "I told our boss that I had two friends who had worked with candidate A before, and that they told me about rumors that candidate A stole direct reports' work products and claimed authorship. I said, of course, I don't want to destroy anyone's reputation but I just never had a good feeling about this person. Then I said that the other finalist had stellar credentials and I think we should move forward with that one. When my boss said that I was alone in my preference, I claimed that sometimes the minority perspective needs to be heard. I knew the word 'minority' would get attention because everyone around here freaks out when you say 'Hey, just because I'm the only one doesn't mean I'm wrong.' Long story short, I won the battle."

I listened, only nodding. Partly because it made sense not to engage in a dialogue about any of this but mostly because I was too shocked to speak. I struggled to breathe and keep my eyes from popping out of their sockets.

"I guess it's fortunate that your friends gave you the heads up. Right?" I asked, hoping that my instincts were wrong.

Kelly hooted."What friends? What rumors? All bullshit. I just couldn't stand the thought of my colleagues winning this round. I needed to remind them who rules the roost."

Regretting accepting this role under a manipulative and deceitful boss, I considered leaving after the first year. But ultimately, working at this organization was more of a positive than negative experience. I decided that turning my attention outside our department was my best strategy. That, and more alcohol.

THE POSSE

Working with my peers, Nico, Rene, and Misha, convinced me to stick it out at this company. These three are brilliant, great collaborators, and My People. We did some groundbreaking work together and established deep connections to each other. I'm still close to them and Rene works for me today.

Nico was on my peer team. Initially, we bonded over the Kelly situation, but quickly realized just focusing on the problem was unproductive and draining. We decided not to let one lousy person fuck up our careers, so we put our heads together to find a solution. Of course, we understood that we were tiptoeing through minefields and things could blow up and Kelly could fire us at any moment. So, our strategy was safety in numbers and high visibility.

Like me, Nico had been on sports teams and had the mindset of focus, game plans, results and we are in this together. They had an upbeat and straightforward style that was magnetic. People all over the company sought them out to participate in new projects or just to be a sounding board. Nico's presence and track record gave them street cred which translated into loads of informal authority. They were generous with their time, feedback, and support. Senior leaders tried to poach Nico away from Kelly, but you can guess how that went.

Nico introduced me to Rene, a senior director, who was in a different department and had a great boss. Our functions didn't overlap much but we shared the same ambitions and outlook. What struck me the most about Rene was how genuine and down-to-earth they were. No pretense, low ego, smart without making you feel dumb, enthusiastic and always curious. They were curious about you, life, ideas, new stuff, things outside the walls of the company. They listened deeply, wanted to know your story and made you feel like the most fascinating person ever.

The three of us had lunch together on Tuesdays. One week, Rene brought Misha. At that time, Nico and I only knew of Misha. Rene had a new idea. "I've been talking with Misha about the new community service initiative they are planning. We've been shooting around some ideas and decided to take an inside and outside approach; bringing the community to the headquarters for training workshops and our employees going out into the neighborhoods to participate in three established volunteer centers. I would love for the two of you to join us in the planning and rollout."

Let me hit the pause button. Understand that, at this point in time, we all had full plates. Working under Kelly ensured that I never had a moment to relax. Now was not the time to take on a window dressing project. Nico was in the same boat. But Rene was unnaturally charming. Without fail, when they made a proposal, our answer was always "sign me up". We couldn't say no. Fortunately, Rene only approached us with winning ideas.

Okay, back to lunch. I spoke first. "Hmmm. Sounds interesting. Misha, how does this tie in with your job and how did you get Rene involved?" Misha described their job and that Rene's department was sponsoring this effort. They had worked with Rene before, their kids went to school together, and they were pals. In other words, Rene couldn't say no to *Misha*! Impressive. They had out-Rene-ed Rene.

Nico was laughing their ass off. We said yes because we wanted to get to know Misha. We hoped that this initiative would provide the fun and stimulation we lacked in our department.

I'll give you the short version of what happened. The four of us were like live wires sparking more ideas than we could manage. We laughed, worked hard, pushed back on each other, brought up ideas, let go of ideas, lost steam, got back on track and, ultimately, came up with a fucking amazing program. It didn't remotely resemble the idea Rene and Misha had floated over that first lunch. When we made our presentation to the executive team for their sign off, we knew we had killed it. Minus the usual cynics, we got high praise from the rest of the team. Misha was even able to finagle Rene, Nico and I being relieved of some of our day job duties to help launch and implement the program. Naturally, Kelly was fuming about this but they could hardly say no to the CEO.

The program was so successful that it caught the attention of other companies in our city. Our merry band toured the city giving presentations and spoke with the media. We made a difference and had a good time doing it.

This project encapsulated everything I wanted for my career. I was working alongside people I felt connected to who were talented, positive, honest and humble. This was my dream team moment. Four people with different backgrounds and skills coming together to create something that no one or two of us could have done alone. Collaboration was exciting, ideas flowed and objectives provided guardrails. It didn't require stopping everything else to participate in this project. When you are having fun, you find the time by becoming more efficient at other stuff. I learned how to say no and to put some boundaries around unreasonable requests. Most importantly, having a meaningful purpose does something for the soul. It's not enough to make cool things or rack up the bonuses. That's good, but not enough. When I don't have work or interests that make the world a little bit better, I get very existential. Is this all there is?

I still keep a picture of the four of us and a newspaper article about the initiative framed in my office. It is a reminder to myself of the four things I mentioned above. Truth be told, I wasn't so clear about the value of that experience at the time. I was riding a sugar high and thought not even Kelly could bring me down. Until they did. More about that later.

SANTANA,
THE TRUTH TELLER

After knocking it out of the park on the community service project, the higher-ups identified me as a "high potential" or HIPO. As in sharp as a hypo-dermic needle or the potential to get high? Both could apply. I was glad about this development because it meant I was on the senior leaders' radar. In the wake of the high profile project, Kelly had to put my name forward and they knew better than to badmouth me.

The eight-month program consisted of three parts; management training classes, cohort support groups and a mentor. Overall, the courses were basic (giving and receiving feedback, supervising others' work, handling conflict) with little guidance about how to apply them to reality. I met some great folks in my group where the conversations were more honest but not helpful beyond letting off steam. Meeting my mentor, Santana, ultimately proved the most valuable part of the experience. But I didn't know that at the beginning.

During the program, I played it safe with Santana. I was doing well despite Kelly's tyranny and I didn't want to blow it. Mostly we talked about how to apply what I was learning to the real situations with my team, department, and boss. I always framed things as "how can I improve myself" which was both the right thing *and* the safe thing to do. Santana offered good guidance that I usually followed. They were smart, successful, and supportive.

Towards the end of the program, it was time for my performance review and a probable promotion. I checked all the boxes and expected the conversation to go well. I had spent the salary bump five times over in my head before I walked into Kelly's office for our discussion. They opened the dialogue with, "So, Micah, how do you think you are doing here?"

I responded with the truth. "I think the past year has gone quite well. My team is functioning better, we are exceeding most targets, the community service initiative was a huge success, and I've been learning so much from the HIPO program."

Kelly smirked. How could I have been so fucking stupid? Leaning forward with too much glee, Kelly declared, "Your team is *not* doing well. Several members have complained that you force them to share uncomfortable personal information. This violates our corporate norms. Neither the team nor you have met expectations on your goals and that has dragged down the department's performance. People think you are distracted by the community project and the HIPO program, and as a result, you have destroyed your reputation as a great collaborator. I've received feedback that you like the limelight too much. Obviously, all this adds up to not getting that promotion. You will need to come back to earth and focus on the right things before I can consider any new position for you."

And there it was. Kelly's revenge for upstaging them. It was going to be impossible to ascend while under their thumb. Fuck! I got out of their office as quickly as possible and barged into my mentor's. Fortunately, Santana was available.

I closed the door and told them the story and then pummeled them with questions. Am I ever going to succeed here or will Kelly blackball me forever? Was there something I did wrong? Which reality was true: the one Kelly put forward or the one I experienced? I punctuated my list with the one burning question I had since I started working here. *Why the fuck hasn't Kelly been fired already?*

Spent but still pissed, I finally stopped talking. Santana took a deep breath and said, "You are not the first person this has happened to. Other talented people were hired into Kelly's group who are no longer there. Two couldn't take it and left the company. One person made a lateral move to another department. Two were fired. And one person was moved up to run another department and is doing fine. That person is me."

I was gobsmacked. My mouth got dry from hanging open. I wanted to know absolutely everything. Santana was forthright at this point. "To answer your last question, Kelly manages the CEO so cunningly that job security for them seems secure. I assume the day will come when the blinders fall away and other people stop protecting the CEO from the truth. The CEO is decent and will be pissed when they find out that Kelly has been playing them. Right now, the dynamics are a bit delicate but the day of reckoning will occur."

Santana's story validated my experience. Now I trusted that they were my ally. We discussed how to handle the situation. The plan was simple: keep my head down, continue to work hard with my team and peers, and Santana would advocate behind the scenes for me. We agreed to extend our mentoring sessions indefinitely so I could get the necessary support.

Returning home that night, a familiar question reemerged: was it worth staying at this company? In one performance review, Kelly destroyed my positive self-perception. When we spoke earlier that day, Santana said that we all get the boss from hell and, if we have the stamina, that trying experience will teach us the most about being a good leader. That rang true but I needed to decide how masochistic I could be. I now had meaningful connections to people, including Santana, who could help me get through this. As I munched on another take-out meal and sipped on a stiff drink, I made a resolution. I was going to develop a new superpower. I was going to become Micah the dragon slayer.

QUINN,
THE NUMERICALLY
FLUENT

Lo and behold, thanks to Santana's behind-the-scenes magic and my continued dedication to my role, six months later I was promoted into a new department. My new boss, Quinn, was nothing like Kelly but I was still gun shy and proceeded with caution. Quinn was a classic company person; politically savvy, focused on numbers and performance, ambitious without being sharp elbowed, cooperative up to a point, not much of a micro-manager, demanding but not punishing. There was a simplicity to our interactions in those first months that made me realize how much time I had spent watching my back with Kelly. I began taking on-line quizzes about PTSD and discovered I was in the throes of recovering from an abusive relationship. I don't want to disrespect folks who have suffered unimaginable harm but the absence of constant anxiety and hypervigilance was profound. My shoulders were relaxed, I walked down the halls without my eyes darting everywhere and I stopped playing mental hopscotch to placate a boss.

Quinn was a walking talking spreadsheet; fluent in numbers, but not so much in humans. I swear they recognized people as "1 FTE, pure overhead, $120k" rather than by name. If you met your targets, it was all good. If not, there was hell to pay. It was impossible to form a meaningful connection or conduct something that resembled a dialogue with Quinn. I was never sure if it was because they had inadequate social skills or because they just didn't care for much besides things that could be measured in neat mathematical terms. Either way, I never fully trusted Quinn.

At this point, I had struck a balance between hard and soft skills with a slight edge towards the soft. Which, by the way, is a very fucked up way of thinking about leadership. Hard sounds tough and aggressive. Soft sounds marshmallowy, passive, diminutive. Like the difference between someone who is buffed from daily workouts at the gym and an overweight couch potato. The relative value and aspiration is obvious to all.

But I digress. Since Quinn was not bilingual, I had to brush up on speaking Numerical. I had basic fluency but I still peppered my data with human implications.

For example, Quinn implemented a major cost-cutting, off-shoring, head-chopping initiative before I moved departments; external consultants, thick PowerPoint decks, the whole deal. They invited me to one of the weekly meetings to offer my opinion on a couple questions. At this point, I knew very little about the project so I sat back and listened for the first thirty minutes. Quinn had the room mesmerized by the savings, upside, efficiency, and streamlining. I remember thinking, "I may be missing something here but this sure looks like a whole bunch of smoke and mirrors." I knew that eventually, someone would ask me a direct question. How could I offer an honest opinion without undermining my boss?

While I was still stuck in my head, someone in the room turned to me and asked my general thoughts.

"I'm still digesting the details but I have a sense of what you are trying to accomplish. It looks like a great deal of work has been done to make sure the numbers add up. I know I'm late to the party, but I was wondering how you are going to manage the personnel changes. It looks like 60 people will lose their jobs. Are you working with HR on this? Also, launching this project will be unsettling for other functions. I assume they will worry whether they are the next group to go. What has the team been doing to anticipate the fallout?"

Dead silence. Then Quinn said, "We have been so focused on business processes, cost cutting, and best practices that we forgot to factor in human resources. Good catch, Micah."

Others chimed in to support Quinn's position but it mostly sounded like hommina-hommina to me. I did not anticipate Quinn's next move. "Since your awareness about the people issues is so keen, Micah, I'd like you to be our liaison to HR to hammer out a plan moving forward. Please have details for the affected group as well as a larger change management strategy for the organization ready in three weeks." Translation: if you are going to be such a smarty pants in a public setting, there will be a price to pay.

From then on, I understood that unless I wanted to take on any huge new projects, I should not challenge Quinn in front of others. They had ambitions and thought the road to success was paved with Trolling for Dollars initiatives. The execs liked the bottom line savings and Quinn did have favored child status. When I felt strongly that a project would harm the culture, I spoke up, knowing that would mean more work for me. Quinn and I developed a symbiosis; my contributions made them look like a more complete leader, and I learned how to speak fluent Numbers.

WHEN LIFE HAPPENS

Just as I was settling into my new role, my significant other dumped me. We had been together for four years, I thought everything was fine except for a few minor glitches, and that life would roll merrily along. Fuck! I didn't need this personally or professionally. I was a mess. Angry, hurt, vengeful, confused, sad. I did a shitty job coping and lashed out or retreated. If I wasn't careful, I could create a Career Altering Moment. After weeks of randomly popping off at my colleagues or "working from home" (aka sleeping most of the day and not showering), Rene intervened. We met after work for happy hour, and over my beer, I ranted about my ex. Rene waited for me to end my harangue and cut to the chase. "Micah, I'm sorry that things fell apart. I can see that you are in pain. But you are messing up at work and I'm afraid you are going to do some irreparable damage. How are you going to pull yourself together?"

I lashed out at Rene. "Do you think I can just snap my fingers and move on? Don't you understand that the person I thought I'd make a future with walked out? I thought that you would be more compassionate."

"Sometimes, tough love is the most compassionate response. After two months, you are still wallowing. You need to get your shit together and I think you need help to do that. Not just so you can be okay for right now; shit is going to happen again. That's life. You need to be able to bounce back, process the experience, and try not to perpetuate any of your unhealthy behaviors in the future. Without the tools to do that, you will find yourself in this hole again."

And this is why I valued Rene so much. They didn't take my self-indulgent bullshit. I had been called out in the kindest way possible. I apologized for being an asshole and promised to turn my behavior around. I set up time to see Santana.

I had mixed feelings about baring my soul at work but felt safe enough to open up with Santana. I didn't plan on laying down on the couch and telling the good doctor about my traumatic potty training years but I did need to talk about the vulnerable state I was in. I felt uncomfortable and nervous; all signs that I needed to take the leap.

"I've been going through a rough patch in my personal life and it's spilling over into how I am at work," I began. "I'm trying to recover from an unexpected break-up but I'm not doing such a good job. I've gotten some feedback from colleagues that I'm on the verge of blowing up my career. I just can't afford to do that. I was hoping you could offer some guidance about how to cope. What do people do when they are an emotional mess and still have to perform at work the next day?"

"First of all, let me say how sorry I am about your break-up." Santana sat down beside me on the couch in their office. "That must be so painful. And I know how tough it is to put away personal issues when you come to work. Emotions can't be switched on and off at will. So, we need to learn ways of managing and integrating what life doles out.

"I was a Director when my father died. We had a difficult relationship so his death brought up a miasma of emotion. Like you, I wasn't very good at compartmentalizing when I got to work. I had a male boss at the time. He tried to be sympathetic, but warned me that I needed to shape up. Furious, I called my best friend that evening to complain, but instead of validating my ire, they offered a new perspective on things. They told me that I have screwed up reactions to men in authority positions; I see them as my distant and cold father and that I will do anything for their approval. If I didn't resolve these emotional issues, they assured me that I would jeopardize my career. If this insight hadn't come from my best friend I would have denied every-thing. This person knew me and had seen me interact with my father. I hated hearing this but it rang true. So I saw a therapist for a while."

Once again, Santana surprised the shit out of me. They consistently challenged me to look at myself, be a complete human being and to grow the fuck up. Always grow. I wanted to know more of the story.

"Tell me how you managed to get a grip on these unconscious reac-tions?"

Santana let out a big laugh. "That's a funny story. I did all this seri-ous work in therapy but I couldn't consistently stop reenacting my dynamic with my father. Then one day I was looking on YouTube for a particular episode of an old sitcom when the suggested next video was a show called *The Dinosaurs*. The daddy dinosaur keeps trying to bond with his baby son. But the baby keeps saying, "Not the Mama. Not the Mama" over and over every time the dad comes near him. I cracked up and developed a habit of telling myself "Not the Papa. Not the Papa" every time I felt my emotions surface about my male bosses. It sure lightens up the moment, but also, it reminds me that the person in front of me is not my father. After some time, I was good to go. No reminders needed."

Maybe I had misjudged Santana. Maybe they were a square peg too. I made a note to myself to find *The Dinosaurs* on YouTube.

Santana stopped laughing to themself and looked at me with a new level of earnestness. "Micah, we are only human and we need our whole selves to show up to work. Learning how to understand and cope with our feelings makes life go more smoothly. It makes us able to pick ourselves up when we stumble and helps us appreciate the moments of great achievement. It makes us more compassionate towards others. In our personal and professional lives, we need to develop some core strengths to be flexible and resilient. People who don't develop that foundation blame others for their shortcomings, alienate or hurt others, take rigid positions, play the victim. The choice is to be conscious, self-aware and strong or scared, angry and fragile. You are at a point in your career and life when it makes sense to wrestle with this decision."

Loads of food for thought. Like, two bowls of pasta, half a pizza and chocolate cake. I thought about Kelly; the quintessential unconscious person with no intention of taking responsibility for their own shit. Although they played tough and hard-assed, I bet they were fragile on the inside. I thought about Saku, Nico, and Rene; grounded, responsible, compassionate, and humble. I needed to take care of my shit or else I would turn into one of those Don't Do That people.

I decided to take Santana's advice and got my butt into therapy. I got just enough help to set me straight, gained some insight, stopped spewing unmanageable feelings at work, and became a more decent person in general. In other words: a work in progress.

THE VANISHING ACT

My peer team was smart, committed and more easily collaborative than my last team. They taught me how to understand and work with Quinn; always lead with the numbers, highlight projected results, and describe how I am going to resolve any obstacles. I tend to live in the world of dialogue and they urged me to get comfortable with monologues.

Before meeting this group, I had it in my head that the best teams felt connected to each other at a supportive or caring level. Not so this team. They were diligent and focused on just getting shit done. Although we worked together for a couple years, I knew very little about them. There was no hanging out at the bar after work or even lunch in the cafeteria. This was unsettling at first and I violated the norms early on. But as I realized that this was a heads-down and respectful group of people, I followed suit. We were efficient, helpful and collaborative. I came to value that sometimes it is enough to be a work group instead of a team with more connective tissue. When I had the itch to do something more creative or challenging, I sought out my buddies Nico, Rene, and Misha.

I noticed in my initial one-on-one meetings with my direct report team in this department that they seemed wary of me. They held back and told me what they thought I wanted to hear. When I asked questions about what they would like from the team experience, I got monosyllabic responses. I tried retreats, get togethers, and new rewards, but without success. I wondered if I'd lost my charm but knew that couldn't possibly be the case.

At one of our Tuesday lunches, I asked the gang for help with my team challenge. Rene offered, "I've heard that Quinn casts a spell on folks. If you shape yourself into their mold, they will help you go far. If you assert independence, you won't last."

"It can't be that bad. You make it sound like people become robots."

"Micah, come on. Tell me you haven't noticed the extreme conformity in your department," Nico asked.

A light bulb went off. I *had* noticed that everyone was partial to white shirts. In fact, I remember feeling so odd when I wore blue one day that I reshuffled my closet that night putting all the white shirts up front. Sitting at lunch I realized that I had never seen Quinn in anything other than a white shirt. OMG! I had transformed without even being conscious of it. Scared the shit out of me. If I could change my wardrobe so mindlessly, what was next?

They all warned me to be careful. "Stick to the norms with your peers and team but don't lose yourself. If you do, we'll have to arrange an intervention to deprogram you!" I laughed with them and told myself I was too strong willed to cave.

Well, that was a bunch of blinding bullshit. The truth was I turned into a total data freak. I developed Quinn's habits of seeing people as overhead and speaking in Excel. I drove my team to perform better than projections which they did most of the time. When they slipped up, I was tough without being nasty. I stopped caring all that much about them and heard their complaints as whining. Although I had moments of self-doubt, I felt less drained at the end of the day. There was less take-out food and more leisurely sit down meals.

Quinn loved all the outstanding results. They gave me stellar reviews, I got a hefty raise, and the CEO knew my name. But Nico, Rene, and Misha were worried about me. They claimed they didn't recognize me anymore. I avoided our lunch dates and made it clear to them that I was only doing what I needed to survive. The answer to their chorus of "Yes, but at what cost?" was "A down payment on a condo." Glares all around.

Deep down, I knew that my friends were right. I couldn't believe that I had changed so thoroughly. I rationalized the transformation in all sorts of nutty ways and concluded that, as long as I worked for Quinn, I didn't have a choice in the matter. Not only had I lost myself, but my friends vanished, too.

During this dark period, I collaborated on a few projects with an EVP named Jessie. Jessie brought out some of my better qualities that had receded under Quinn's reign. As an added bonus, Jessie was bilingual and spoke both Excel and Human fluently. They talked about their team members and gave them credit for their contributions to the initiatives. Jessie invested in people and didn't need the spotlight.

During one of our check-in meetings, Jessie asked, "Who on your team is helping on this project?" I ignored the question and continued to go through the spreadsheet. They stopped me. "Micah, I can't believe that you've done all this work yourself. I know you had help. I'd like to know their names."

I waved my hand and unloaded. "They would be nowhere if it weren't for my drive."

"Micah, I respect you and think you have the potential to go far.

But not if you maintain this attitude. No one rises to the top without acknowledging the great people that contributed to the success. The more you feature yourself and not others, the more you risk going down in flames. There is already talk about you derailing your career because of your growing self-importance."

If I didn't like Jessie so much I would have dismissed everything they said. I should have heeded the guidance. Instead I tucked it away. I did look at myself in the mirror and realized I needed a haircut. But that was about all.

The more I became a hardass, the more I pleased Quinn. And the more I pleased Quinn, the more isolated I became. My friends refused to eat with me, two direct reports left the company, my peers avoided me and even my family left me alone. I had the trappings of outward success but I had to admit that I was depressed.

By now you must be thinking the situation was so fucked up that I got fired. Almost.

Quinn had dangled the carrot of a promotion to VP and I told myself that I would come to my senses when that happened. When they called me in for a talk I felt cautiously optimistic. But I was no longer the gullible Charlie Brown. I had experience with that damn football!

"Micah, we find ourselves in an unfortunate position," Quinn began. "As much as I am thrilled with your progress and performance, I had a visit from HR last week. They conducted exit interviews with your two staff members who left recently. It seems your attitude and behavior was just this side of abusive, which prompted HR to speak with some other folks to get the lowdown on you. People praised you for your diligence and results, but they also complained that you can be cold and dismissive of others."

While Quinn was reciting my misdeeds, I kept thinking, shit, I'm getting fired. Shit, I should have listened to my posse. Shit, I can't even blame someone else. Shit, how will I pay my mortgage?

Quinn continued. "After much discussion with HR and others, we determined that you are worth saving. Your history here has been very positive and you have been on everyone's radar. But in the past couple years, you've stopped being a good collaborator, you've stopped developing your team, and shifted your focus solely to yourself, to everyone's detriment. We want the old Micah back."

It was all I could do not to scream "I'll tell you what changed! You became my boss and turned me into an automaton." That's just the printable stuff. Use your imagination.

"We agreed to get you a leadership coach for six months. You need to turn it around. If you make meaningful changes during that time, you are safe. If not, you will be dismissed. Personally, I'd hate to lose you. You've got all the right stuff and I am confident you can make this right. Are you willing to commit to doing this work?"

Reflexively, I said all the right things, we shook hands and I left the office early. I was furious and stunned. I modeled my behavior after Quinn and I didn't see anyone calling them on the carpet. I considered sending hateful texts to those two weasels or taking a long (fast) drive or pounding it out at the gym or giving HR a piece of my mind. I opted for an Uber ride home and a stiff drink. Then I googled "edible crow" in preparation for seeing Nico, Rene and Misha at lunch the next day.

Once the shock wore off, I had a conversation with Jessie. I ate more shit as I told them the story. That's what being humbled will do to you. I wanted to know what Jessie thought about this whole coaching thing. This was different than a mentor, which seemed like a reward. Coaching seemed like a punishment.

Jessie smirked. "Do you want to know what the first words out of my mouth were when I met my coach? I said I'm such a fucking asshole and I'm going to lose my job because of that."

Jessie? An asshole? They had a coach? I just couldn't imagine this person sitting in front of me being "that person". I wanted to know everything.

Jessie told me the saga of how they lost their way. The more I listened, the more I felt I was finally looking in that goddamn mirror.

To succeed, Jessie thought they needed to shape shift. The problem was there was so much shifting that it was an invasion of the body snatchers. A force took over and Jessie was nowhere to be found.

"I got so much out of the coaching experience that I met with that person for a year and a half. The urgent changes happened quickly and I knew I was out of the woods. My big question was: how did I let this happen and how can I never let it happen again? I can do the numbers as well as anyone but I'm primarily a people person. Erring on that side will always work out well in the end for the results *and* the human beings. Also, I figured out some psychological triggers that cause me to mold myself in my boss' image instead of being my own person. I no longer fear rejection or disappointment or dismissal from a senior person. If how I operate doesn't suit the powers that be, then I'm probably in the wrong place. Lastly, it is not about me, me, me. Being self-confident is good. Being self-centered is not. If you thought you were such hot shit, you will have loads of time in your own company."

I realized that beyond most executives' cardboard cut-out image was a real multi-dimensional person. Even the good ones screwed up. Maybe all folks on the rise have their comeuppance. It's what you do with those dark moments that foretells what happens next. I left Jessie's office with complete resolve. I was going to reacquaint myself with myself, learn as much as I could, and let the chips fall where they may. When I got home I headed straight for the mirror. Staring back at me was someone I understood was no longer the fairest of them all.

SYDNEY,
THE VOICE OF
REASON

During my first meeting with my coach, Sydney, I pulled a Jessie. Without knowing this person from Adam, I blurted out, "I've lost my soul. Can you help me find it? I seem to have replaced it with a lump of cold, hard coal. Whether or not I get fired, this just isn't working for me." I rambled for ten minutes; a combination of self-flagellation and the-devil-made-me-do-it.

After listening with an inscrutable expression to my plaintive rant, Sydney grinned. "Feel better? Seems like you needed to get that off your chest."

"Oh shit! I should have asked about confidentiality before I let loose. What are the rules here? How will we spend our time? Will my boss get reports about our conversations? Can you fix me?"

Sydney reassured me that our sessions were confidential and that we would work on specific goals related to the changes I wanted to make. They described how coaching works and what each of us needed to do to make it a success. "This isn't therapy. It's more private and reflective than mentoring. A mentor is someone inside the company and a coach is someone outside the company, so we have different perspectives. I primarily focus on your development as a leader and the organization provides important context. A mentor helps you understand the organization so that you can tailor your growth as a leader accordingly. As you say, whether or not you get fired, you want to be your best self. You want to take up residence in your core again. That's our game plan."

Our first order of business was to identify my shitty behaviors, figure out where they came from, understand them at a deep level, and make changes. We were aiming for real and permanent change so success hinged on my being honest with myself. I didn't always love this process. I hadn't spent much time being this introspective and I found it awkward. Sydney forced me to answer hard questions like "Why do you think you became so cold towards others?" and "Do you think you need to act a certain way to be successful even when it is at odds with your natural tendencies?" Before our sessions, I never thought about this stuff. As we delved deeper, I grew more curious about my own psychology. I uncovered some abiding strengths that I was quite familiar with and learned about blind spots that sent my ego (boastful, indifferent to others' feelings) or id (impulsive, unthinking) into a frenzy. These conversations also helped me to understand other people better. Even though I excelled at reading people, being more honest with myself caused me to be less critical of others. Funny how that works.

I learned some things in this work with Sydney that became building blocks for my growth as a leader. Brace yourself for another list. First, I'm used to things coming easy for me so when they don't I get frustrated in some fairly ugly ways. Take my team as an example. I tried and tried my best to do all the right things but it didn't result in the group coming together in ways I expected. So, what did I do? I got angry at *them* and shut down. I never asked *myself* what I was doing wrong. I never considered that I was part of the problem. Second, I drank my boss and the company's Kool-Aid. Funny thing is, I never saw myself as a conformist. Square peg and all. I minimized this transformation in my own mind. What Sydney helped me understand is that we human beings are susceptible to joining the pack to survive. If that is true, I inquired, then why did I resist Kelly so well but not Quinn? It turns out we are all quite primitive. I accurately perceived Kelly as a danger and protected myself through avoidance and finding support elsewhere. Quinn was not the same threat so I relaxed and then, voila, glug-glug-glug. Third, it's easy to dehumanize others when I am less human myself. The more robotic, cold, distant, analytic, perfectionistic, demanding and uncivil my behavior became, the hollower I was as a person. And last, when I stop listening to my own inner voice (crazy though it can be at times) and the well-meaning guidance from those I trust, I'm in deep doo-doo. My posse had tried to save me but I was unresponsive. There was significant pain in their abandonment but it was all on me. I was a resistant asshole. The fucked up rationales I told myself about why I was acting so differently were just that; fucked up. This might be the most troubling and dangerous thing I learned from the coaching: I gave up my good sense and power because I let my ambitions run wild. I let Quinn take the wheel. Just remembering that now still makes me shudder. I made a vow to myself that if my friends sound the alarm, I must give them priority and control because it would indicate that I was already out of my mind. Friends don't let friends disappear from themselves!

Armed with these insights, I begged Nico, Rene, and Misha for a second chance. High fives all around. Phew! I had heart-to-hearts with my team members individually and as a group. I offered a sincere mea culpa, asked for direct feedback and promised to work with them to make significant changes to our team. They were caught off guard by my apology which allowed them to be quite candid. I did not like hearing what they said but I listened respectfully. Things didn't change overnight, but this was a step in the right direction.

Recalibrating my relationship with my boss was trickier. I stopped kissing Quinn's ass, challenged them on important issues, spoke more frequently about people issues and just became more Micah. I even began joking with Quinn which, as it turns out, they really enjoyed.

I threw myself into another high-visibility project with some new colleagues as part of my redemption tour. I proved that I was, once again, a good collaborator and not made of stone. I kept a low profile and put the spotlight on others. I felt like I was back in my own skin again and when I looked in the mirror I recognized that face staring back at me.

My superiors deemed the coaching a resounding success and they promoted me. This moment felt sweeter than others because I had to work for this one. I was beginning to realize that it's okay if everything doesn't come easy. In fact, struggling meant that I was learning and growing.

SHAKE UPS AND
SHAKE DOWNS

Shortly after my promotion, Nico decided to leave. Kelly had crushed Nico's spirit so much that the decision was ultimately an easy one. Our gang celebrated their new job and promised to have regular drinks together once a month. We have stayed close all these years. We often reflect upon how, during those years at that company, we learned what great leadership does and does not look like and how it can help or damage people. P.S. Nico became a CEO too.

After continued success and developing a reputation as a talent magnet, Saku was terminated. That was odd enough but the explanation for it was worse. "Saku just doesn't have that extra something. Not aggressive enough. We don't see them as senior leadership material." What the fuck?! I sat down with Jessie after I heard the news and asked how to possibly make sense of that one.

"I tried to advocate on Saku's behalf but it went nowhere. If you step back and see what traits most of the executives have, there is a pattern. Tough, distant, demanding, command and control. Saku achieved results with a different style. They put up with me and Santana but that may not last forever, either."

"Why don't you leave and find someplace that shares your values? Doesn't it make you crazy?"

"Some days I feel they leave me alone to do my own thing so it's fine. Other days, it just feels too lonely. I don't know how many more rodeos I have left in me, so it might be easier to stay."

I could feel Jessie's exhaustion and wondered if I was looking at my future. Were all companies so life-sucking? Did all companies favor an inhumane form of leadership? Would great leadership role models always be the exception rather than the rule? I had pulled myself back from the abyss. But for what? These "meaning of life" questions hurt my brain. Time for a good meal and a nice glass of wine.

When the next red flashing light blinked in my eyes, I was more prepared. An EVP reached out to me for feedback about Quinn. It was part of the succession planning process and Quinn was being considered for an opening at the Big Table. Rather than reflexively spewing about Quinn, I played it very chill.

"How can I be most helpful? What specifically are you looking for," I asked.

"I would like to know about Quinn's willingness to work with others, their strengths and any developmental needs you see."

I was my most diplomatic self. "I have learned a great deal from Quinn about how to look at the business and assess new opportunities. That may be their biggest strength. They give me a good deal of latitude and support to achieve my goals without a lot of microman-agement. I don't know how to respond fully to your question about development needs. If the executive team requires extensive col-laboration or team work, there may be some gaps." I tried to give an alert without slamming Quinn.

They asked me to explain what kind of gaps. "I think most of us in the department understand that Quinn is very ambitious and wants to do the right thing for the company. Sometimes that comes at other people's expense. Quinn doesn't sufficiently acknowledge others' contributions and I don't always trust Quinn. But, I imagine that an executive team is a different beast so this might not be relevant."

I kept the conversation as brief as possible. When I heard that Quinn was promoted I wasn't surprised. By this time, I fully understood the politics of the place and what they valued. I also began taking every recruiter's call. I didn't want to look in the mirror again and see Jessie's face looking back at me.

A FRESH START ...

The next stop on my adventure was as a VP at a new company. This time, I did a better job researching the company and displayed more of my true nature in the interviews. More self-aware and confident, I figured that if people didn't want me as I was then I wasn't going to twist myself into a pretzel to suit them. After all, the real Micah was absolutely fabulous.

When I met with Chris, the EVP who would be my boss, I laid my cards on the table. I talked about what I learned from the past good times but revealed more about the painful lessons of the bad times. My bottom line: I wouldn't mirror my boss's behavior and if Chris wanted a lap dog, it wasn't me. In turn, Chris told me about the executive team's push to change the culture in the last year. They were serious about becoming more people-centric. To achieve this, they had encouraged new executive behaviors, inclusion programs, new reward systems, monthly "Ask the CEO" forums, and new team training. Chris did not over sell their progress and explicitly warned me about the push-pull between the new and the old way of doing things. But the CEO was committed and doing everything possible to model the shift. Hiring new leaders was one strategy to implement the changes.

I'll admit, I wondered where I put my superpower cape because this job had Micah written all over it. But in my head, I heard Sydney saying, "Get over yourself! You are insufferable!" So, I accepted the position from a humbler space and sighed with relief. My journey to the dark side left me drained and I looked forward to a fresh start. In my compensation negotiations, I insisted that the company pay for a coach. It was chump change for them and aligned with the new culture push, and I didn't fully trust myself. Having a coach would ensure that my next mistakes would suck a lot less. Sydney was happy to come along for the ride.

I had one major goal as I stepped into this new opportunity: use what I had learned to be a better leader and to bring out the best in others. It was time to step up my game.

... AND A NEW TEAM

I was determined to build an incredible team so I changed my strategy. I scheduled a two-hour meeting with each person so I could begin building rapport. I asked about their backgrounds, experience, achievements, concerns and what they wished they could do but weren't being asked to do. I also wanted to hear what they thought of the changing culture agenda. By going deeper than "so, tell me about your job", I learned several things: what were the untapped resources, where was the diversity of perspectives, who was ready for change (or not), what mattered and how did they get along together. I also discovered who was comfortable having a dialogue. Who asked me questions, who needed to be prodded to express themselves, who demonstrated curiosity about what comes next, who had ideas. Armed with this information, I planned our first team offsite. I hoped to deepen connections and encourage the team to interact around real work issues.

I started with something simple.

Me: You have all shared with me privately some hidden talent, idea or aspiration you wish you could use at work. I'd like everyone to share that openly so we can all know what untapped resources we have.
Billie: I'd love our team to lead a green initiative for the company.
Sami: I don't think you guys know that I can code. It would be cool if that was needed on some project.

Rory: I used to do a lot of project management at my last job. I'd like to do some of that again.
Cary: What you see is what you get.
Frances: I prefer to work as a team on almost everything. If it's not always possible, I'd at least like to collaborate with one or two of you.
Riley: I play the guitar.
Alex: I train for marathons in my free time. I find the discipline I use to get ready for a race is the same stuff I do to manage a big project.
Gael: I don't know how to say no and that gets me overwhelmed or behind sometimes. I would like to ask the team's help on this.
Jia: I'd love to have monthly Big Thinking sessions. For two hours, we'd reflect on the value of what we are doing, how to make it more meaningful and what new ideas we should pursue.

Over the course of the retreat it became clear that Riley and Cary were dead weight. I wavered about whether Rory and Sami might be coachable.

The following week I had serious conversations with Riley and Cary outlining my expectations, asking how I could help them succeed and about their commitment to step up. I also warned them what would happen if they bombed, giving them three months to turn it around. I was a badass without being a shithead. I also met with Rory and Sami to create development plans and made it clear that I needed more out of them and that I would support their efforts. The rest was up to them. They were anxious but willing to work hard. I was still a badass but with more compassion.

This go around I spent more one-on-one time with my team members. I realized that I had been too lax about this before, letting cancellations pile up and eventually no meetings whatsoever. I made every other week check-ins sacrosanct on both sides. No one could cancel or postpone unless it was urgent. That rule applied to myself most of all. You know, model what you mean or no one will follow suit. I needed to prove that they could trust me.

At my last job, I learned that if my behavior wasn't consistent, then there was no chance in hell that my team would trust me. I remember Lee, the Senior Director, at my first big job. The one who was in the military. They described how leaders must always be in the trenches with their troops modeling what is needed otherwise the whole group lags behind. It took me this long, but I finally got what Lee was saying. I vowed to keep a visual image of them in my mind as I sorted out this team. The picture in my brain included me in camo with a heavy backpack following Lee on an obstacle course cursing all the way.

My two losers flamed out and Rory just couldn't cut it no matter how hard they tried. I unceremoniously fired Riley and Cary and found a different position in the company that suited Rory better. With help from members of my team, I promoted two gems from other departments into our group. A win-win all around.

Or so I thought. As I saw it, I was carrying out this new culture plan; holding people to high standards, helping them achieve, replacing them if they fail, and promoting from within. Chris supported my actions but they warned me that some on the leadership team were unhappy. They felt I had rushed in like gangbusters and upset the status quo. And, as it turns out, some thought Riley was a rising star. Fuck.

I wanted to understand how serious the executive team was about making the real changes they gave lip service to. Did I now have a demerit for doing what I was hired to do or was I being set up to take the fall for an ill-conceived or window-dressing culture transformation?

Chris gave a knowing smile. "I understand why you feel skeptical about this culture initiative. Your questions are legitimate. The CEO and many of the executives are committed and anticipate the pain or pushback that comes with this sort of transformation. Others are struggling. They were successful under the old set of rules and they worry the CEO will replace them. I don't see evidence of that but I get why they are concerned. If they continue to resist making personal or department changes, I'm not sure what the CEO will do."

"That's a helpful perspective," I replied. "But I still don't know where that leaves me. It sounds like my detractors have job security that I haven't accrued yet."

"Let me worry about them. You keep doing what you know is right. In the meantime, people with your values continue moving into senior roles. If I had to place a bet, it would be on you."

The heavens parted. The angels sang. This is what a great boss sounds and acts like. I made a giant note-to-self that day. If you know your staff is right, advocate on their behalf and protect them from the riff-raff. Chris told me just enough to reassure me but didn't pull back the curtain too far. I didn't have to get sucked into any palace intrigue or worry about getting dinged. Phew! What a difference it makes when your boss is an honest broker with self-confidence and grace.

This potential hiccup didn't distract me from my zeal to build a great team. But I was more honest with myself about the challenges. I had to admit that, even for someone like me who has some mad people skills, teams are a fucking grind. So many individual needs, variations in performance, big goals to monitor, careers to nurture, tough conversations, inevitable low points, personality clashes on the team. When would I have time to do my own job? When would I get to close my door (I finally had one of those!) and have a moment of peace? I was at the point in my career where I understood more fully the demands of being a leader. I was starting to understand why many leaders suck at the people thing and why some just say, why bother?

At the same time, watching my people develop and do great things, seeing the team come together, demonstrating over and over that collective efforts outshine individual ones every day, experiencing the benefits of supporting each other, achieving those quantum leaps in performance...the pay-off was enormous. Of course, there were countless nights when I came home to binge watch reruns of old soccer matches (with a great beer or two) just to cool my jets. But, on balance, it was worth it.

CHRIS, (FINALLY)
THE GREAT BOSS

Working with Chris was refreshing. I learned a great deal from them that I have integrated into my own leadership style. Chris showed me that committing to the development of your staff makes a huge difference. Just as I had promised to be fully present for my team, Chris gave me consistent attention. That allowed me to ask questions, avoid mistakes before they happened and to be challenged to up my game. I was motivated to exceed performance expectations because I wanted to please them. The praise was addictive. Chris also demonstrated how to create the perfect professional boundaries. I know, very psycho-babble of me. They connected with me without making it too personal. We didn't become chums or go for drinks after work. We only shared personal information if it was relevant, like where we were going on vacations in case we needed to be reached. I never heard about Chris's challenges with the CEO and I never, ever heard shit about others. I did hear tons of praise about people's accomplishments. Chris made it look easy to feel the bond but not get too close.

I obsessively watched Chris manage my peer team to learn as much as possible. I felt I was on a good track with my direct report team but I wanted to see how Chris mastered our group of talented and ambitious folks. We were a motley crew, which made life so much more interesting.

The best thing I learned from Chris about managing a leadership team was how to arrive at consensus. It was fucking masterful. Let's say there was a tough issue the team had to grapple with where consensus was necessary. In the week before the team gathered, Chris met with each of us individually. They started the conversation with, "I'd like to hear your thoughts about Issue X." I would then babble on about my position, why other ideas were crap and describe the amazing outcomes we would see from my brilliant idea. Chris listened carefully, jotted notes, nodded and asked a couple clarifying questions. Once I finished, Chris would paraphrase in one or two sentences what I had said. It awed me that they could distill my deep thoughts into such a simple line or two. What Chris did next was true wizardry. "If I built on your idea and added just a twist here and there, I wonder what you would think of this proposal." Then they would put forward something that sounded like a fantastic embellishment of my core idea. Seeing that I was hooked, Chris closed the deal this way. "So, if I made this proposal in our team meeting, would I get your support?" Two thumbs up from me. When they left my office all I could think was, "I just love working with Chris. They have a way of improving on my already great ideas. I've never felt more validated by a boss before."

I know what you are thinking. What a dense idiot I am. How egotistical. How naive. And you would be right. It's embarrassing to let you know that I worked for Chris for a whole year before I figured out what was really happening here. I still had a bit too much ego for my own good and assumed that all our toughest team decisions were rooted in my cleverness. I didn't realize that my peers felt exactly the same way. Chris listened to our ideas, drew elements from each, and ultimately steered the team to where we needed to go. We each felt invested because we recognized a piece of our own stuff in the mix. Like magic, Chris conjured consensus one-on-one before the team ever convened.

Once I got out of my own way and understood the process, I began to use this with my direct report team. I found it worked especially well with anything that required change. Establishing that private one-on-one rapport is at the crux of effective leadership. Sure, it is nice if you are a razzle dazzle visionary who can inspire groups of people. But nothing quite beats deep curiosity about someone else to create the connections necessary to achieve great things.

GABY, THE
ORGANIZATIONAL
GLUE

I became quite attached to one of my peers, Gaby, a long-term employee with a "Special Projects" role. They had no personal agenda except to turn the keys over to smart people who could grow the company in new ways. I hope you've had the good fortune of working with someone like Gaby; part mentor, part colleague, part consigliore, part person behind the scenes who gets all the super hard issues resolved, part company historian and storyteller. In short, invaluable and selfless. The Glue Person holds things together, explains how to actually get shit done, tells you what to focus on and what is bullshit, squashes rumors (even though they know where all the bodies are buried), constantly roots for you and the company to succeed, speaks truth to power and who you hope never retires. I was lucky that Gaby did not call it quits while I was at this company.

This describes a typical encounter with Gaby. My head would be exploding over…fill in the blank. A person, the politics, some initiative. I'd race into Gaby's office, slam the door and start ranting. Always calm, patient and attentive, Gaby waited until I ran out of steam. They would ask a couple questions: what had I done to resolve the situation, what obstacles did I bump into, what did I think was the right solution. If Gaby felt I hadn't explored all avenues, they recommended a new pathway. If they felt my thinking was wrong headed, they told me straight up. And if they believed I had hit a wall that needed to be breached, they simply said, "I'll see what I can do." To this day, I don't know what magic they performed. All I know is that the right wheels started turning.

Gaby was a rare and unique gift; to me, to the team, to the organization. Some days I wonder if I have what it takes to be the Glue Person for an organization. I think I might have too much ego to work that well behind the scenes. Big sigh.

THE MENTEE BECOMES A MENTOR

Now that I was a senior leader, it was my turn to be a mentor. I was pleased with this development but, between you and me, I was also concerned. My people time was so maxed out that I wasn't sure how much juice I had for this. I also wasn't sure that I could come up with pithy wisdom like my former mentors. I knew I could give good advice but wasn't sure if I was at the Wise Person stage of my own development. Didn't I need to be about 20 years older?

It turns out I didn't need to worry. By my third mentee, I noticed a pattern that was reinforced with each new person I met over the years. Talented people who were moving up in the ranks did not feel safe to be their fullest selves. They felt marginalized, silenced, and/or pressed into conformity. While the company recognized their raw talent, they provided mentors to these individuals to "smooth out the rough edges." Well, I was no piece of fine grit sandpaper so I encouraged them to let more of themselves shine through.

Take Louisa, who told me about some feedback she received from her boss. "You are too direct, emotionally expressive and talk with your hands too much. You need to tone it down." Then she summed up the situation in two crushing sentences. "I'm a Latina working for a white man in a predominantly white company. Will I keep getting critical feedback for being myself?" And there it was. Fuck. I understood what she was saying in my bones. Outside the norm.

Or Rhonda, a brilliant talent with that "it" factor. In one of our sessions, she described a troubling incident. "I was meeting with a couple peers and my boss about a major project. We realized that we needed more resources and decided to hire a contractor. When I suggested using a minority vendor that specializes in our work, my boss said, 'No way. I don't trust that they will provide *qualified* minorities.' I couldn't hold back. I raised my voice and made my position clear. 'You are telling this African American woman that it is hard to find qualified minorities? When was the last time you pressed your favorite vendor to be sure they supply *qualified* white people?' None of my peers spoke up and my boss ended the meeting abruptly. I was called in for a private conversation and was told my anger was inappropriate and out of line and that I better shape up. Now what do I do?" The Big Three: person of color, woman, anger.

I heard many stories about women who had been mistreated. These women found that when they showed up as their fullest selves, they would be called a bitch, or a ball buster, or worse. I told these women that they will be called names even if they are prim and proper ladies so they might as well just be themselves. The mentoring work was to help them turn off those nasty voices that caused the self-censoring. Easier said than done. Reversing a lifetime of female socialization isn't going to happen in six months of mentoring but many women were able to make progress.

From these discussions, I recognized that the push for everyone to blend into the majority (usually white and male) culture was enormous in the company culture. Conformity and uniformity is predictable and maintains the social order. But marginalizing people who are different has a lasting impact. Those individuals are made to feel inferior and they hold back contributions that could make the company and its culture improve. They carry the pain and burden and the organization is less open and creative. In the corporate world, anger is okay for white men. Heaven help you if you are female or brown. Basically, Ginger Rogers was right. A woman can do everything a man does but backwards and in heels...with much less recognition. The standards for women and people of color are tougher than for white men but few people want to acknowledge or change this reality.

Hearing their stories, guiding them to emerge from the shadows and supporting their efforts to be different lit a fire in me. I understood their struggles as a square peg and took up the banner to push this culture change faster than it was taking. One of the new values was to honor and encourage diversity of all kinds, but on the ground, the square pegs were urged to conform rather than to shake up the status quo. I felt I could advocate among top leaders to open their minds while buoying up my mentees. This was not easy.

I became obsessed with the idea of Voice and why certain types of Voices are viewed as threatening in many companies. How can an individual fully express their unique Voice? How can all the different Voices in a team find their harmony together? How can leaders integrate diverse perspectives effectively among the senior Voices? How can an organization ensure that the chorus of different Voices is amplified? How can people go from being most comfortable with conformity to craving variety?

I developed a minor reputation as someone who listened and was willing to be an advocate so I heard many more stories of ethnic and gender discrimination. Most times, I advised people to continue to be themselves and not to twist themselves into an identity that didn't make sense to them. I also urged them to respectfully address each infraction and report it to HR to create a paper trail. If the company was serious about transforming the culture, shit had to change.

But the real change had to happen at the leadership level. I took a page from Chris's playbook. I met one-on-one with my VP peers and some of the EVPs. Once I got passed the inevitable "Of course, I support diversity" lip service, I probed deeper. "What if I told you that people of color feel invisible here? What if I told you that every day they feel less-than?" Everyone I spoke with would whip out the first exception to these problems they could think of and tell me about how they personally had promoted so-and-so. But I kept pushing. When I asked if they felt our leadership group made space for different voices, different styles, or different opinions they had to admit, no, we did not do a good job of that. Then they described how they, too, felt dismissed when they went against the norm. Once they could relate to the situation personally I was able to deliver the punchline. "Just take what you feel and multiply it by 100. That's what women and people of color feel all the time, not just occasionally."

When talking with male peers about gender discrimination they asked, "Why don't women just speak their minds?" Rather than explain, I turned it around on them. "When was the last time you felt you couldn't express your opinion? When was the last time you were told not to get so angry? When was the last time someone spoke over you only to repeat your idea? When was the last time a boss grabbed your ass and leered at you? When was the last time you felt physically unsafe with a colleague? When was the last time you had a performance review where you received feedback that you were too emotional?" At the very least, this got some men to empathize with the experience of women. But reversing a lifetime of male socialization doesn't happen in a few conversations or through a corporate directive.

It was a start. I kept being a pain in the ass in leadership settings. I constantly challenged the need for more Voices in the room or commented on the demographics in the meeting or raised my own oddball ideas. With each pushback, I repeated the company line: We are working towards a culture of greater equity and inclusion. They could hardly call bullshit at that point even if they were thinking it.

How could I be an advocate for change from within without alienating my peers? What would it take for leaders to see the fuller picture and to do more of the right thing? I knew I was already walking a thin line with my colleagues because some were starting to avoid me. They were getting sick of The (stop being such a dick) Talk. So, I shifted tactics. I came to realize that fundamental change about race or gender had to be well informed and personal. Those in power needed to be compassionately moved to lead the change. They needed to develop a deep understanding that discrimination was a human violation. I needed to show them that nothing disastrous would happen to them or the company if they allowed Others an equal share of power. They needed to question and move past the cultural socialization ingrained in their outlooks and behaviors.

I hired a diversity, equity and inclusion vendor that facilitated a series of experiences for the leadership group. They presented a mix of short films, talks, history, research and storytelling to provide information. The other aspect of the work involved more private and safe discussions that allowed individuals to reflect on their biases. How much exposure did they actually have with Others? What was the genesis of their negative beliefs? What were some core personal ideas they didn't want to let go of and why? In the privacy of these conversations, leaders came to understand what was a reflexive response born from bad information.

The shift that occurred during that year felt more like lots of little cracks in the veneer rather than a wholesale transformation. Some leaders saw the light and worked hard to grow. Others were unmoved but didn't show as much resistance as before. Many remained the threatened assholes they always were but this process made it harder for them to retaliate. They took their resentment underground, mainly because the CEO was now fully on board. At the end of one of the leadership inclusion sessions, the CEO was visibly shaken up. With a catch in their voice, they said, "I've considered myself more aware than most when it comes to the harm of stereotypes and discrimination. Today my knowledge moved from my head to my soul. I feel such pain and shame about the gross injustices done to women and people of color. To treat some groups of human beings as "superior" or "inferior" is immoral. We are all human beings. We—I—must do better."

At this point, the CEO removed two of the most resistant executives. That was the beginning of greater momentum for the culture change. You could see and feel the difference in the organizational ethos. Different people were invited to participate in meetings, more people of color were hired, women were promoted, pay equity studies were conducted and corrections made. Some of my mentees described improved work conditions while others had run out of patience and left the company. Change came too slowly for them. Truth be told, my crusade for diversity had a long-term impact on shaping what kind of leader I wanted to be. This was a turning point.

POLITICS AND
BLIND SPOTS

While Chris did a great job of making sure I had direct contact with the CEO and advocated for me, the inclusion program put me in the spotlight and as a result, the CEO sought me out routinely. I felt heard and respected and we came to develop a productive rapport—maybe a little too productive. Despite the new norms of relaxing the hierarchy, Chris felt passed over. The CEO often came to me directly about things that were typically under Chris's purview; an awkward dynamic. Chris started sniping at me and our relationship became tense. Fuck! I was in territory I didn't know how to navigate.

Good thing I negotiated to have leadership coaching when I started at the company; Sydney helped me understand Executive Politics. I had graduated from HiPo to ExPo and I had no confidence I would ever receive my diploma. I sucked (and still suck) at politics. I think it is a nasty game and I don't want to play. But Sydney wouldn't hear it.

"Micah, you need to stop being so naïve. The more you ascend in an organization, the thinner the air gets. When there is less oxygen, everyone scrambles to stay alive," Sydney explained.

"So, there's one oxygen tank and everyone has to pass the mask around? I've heard of cost cutting but that is insane!"

They pressed on. "Once someone attains real power and status, they don't want to lose it. They finally summited Everest and they enjoy the view. But staying on top is as difficult as getting there. It brings up all kinds of questions like, 'Will I drop out of favor with the CEO?', 'Will one of my peers sabotage me?', 'Where am I in the pecking order?', 'How deferential do I need to be?' Or your favorite question, 'How much of my fullest self do I need to tuck away?' If you think you have anxiety as a VP, you might need to double your Xanax prescription as you keep moving up."

"Okay, so how do I maintain a good relationship with Chris while developing a good one with the CEO? How do I stay connected to the CEO without pissing off Chris? My head hurts just thinking about it."

Sydney recommended several strategies to see what worked. The next time the CEO circumvented Chris, I redirected them to consult with Chris instead of me. Nope. I gave Chris a heads up about a meeting I was going to have with the CEO so they wouldn't think I was sneaking around. Nope. As a last resort, I told the CEO that I was uncomfortable cutting Chris out of the loop. I kept the focus on my feelings. They backed off after this and let me know how important it was for Chris and me to continue to work well together. Bingo. Things went back to normal with Chris and I felt a bit smarter about ExPo. A bit, not a lot.

BRIDGING THE
GREAT DIVIDE

In my peer group, Bailey, Charley, and I became thick as thieves. I was still in touch with my old posse and was thrilled to find a new one. We teamed up on inventive initiatives and became the role models for the new culture. We found ourselves in the position of being ostracized by some of the staff and sought after by others.

Over lunch one day, Bailey bitched about their key internal partner. Not a new phenomenon but this time Bailey was on the edge. "I can't take this shit anymore! In public, the EVP says all the right stuff and everyone thinks they are the friggin' second coming. But in our meetings, all we hear about are their glory days. I have heard the story about the big merger they negotiated at least once a month. That deal closed in 1999! Why hasn't the CEO found a retirement strategy for them yet? How can we make significant changes around here when we've got senior leaders stuck in the last century?"

I spent several sessions with Sydney talking about the rift between old and new in the company.

"There is a delicate balance to be struck between honoring and understanding the history of an institution and doing the hard work of refining and updating how it moves forward," Sydney offered. "If you disregard the past you are implying that the values, the people, the hard work, the accomplishments mean nothing. The only thing that matters is right now and the future." Sydney explained to me. "But actually, history is the foundation and jumping off point for the good stuff yet to come. You can't think of today as square one."

"Now you sound like my colleagues who say, 'when I started here we did things differently,' or 'if it ain't broke, don't fix it.' They live in the past and grumble about how different things are today. It feels condescending and like anything valuable happened already and we kids just don't get it. It reminds me of how my grandparents talk about their Vietnam protest days."

"Micah, have you ever asked your grandparents to tell you stories about those years?"

"I never have to. Their description of the 1969 march on Washington is on an instant replay tape. I've heard it over and over again."

"Do you ever ask them questions? Is there anything that makes you curious? Do you just write them off as old school? What is going through your mind when they talk about protesting the war?"

"Mostly I'm thinking I have this story memorized. I'm bored to tears but I love them so I listen respectfully."

"What do you think would happen if you probed for more depth or details? Do you wonder if they felt worried about their safety? Have you asked them how the war touched them so personally that it prompted their actions? Do you see evidence in them today that those years and actions had a lasting impact on who they became? Have you asked them why those days feel so rich and principled and modern times don't? Or have you asked them directly if there is something about today that feels frightening to them personally?"

For someone who sees themself as compassionate and inclusive, Sydney's questions led me to see this blindspot. Fuck.

"Okay, point taken. So, I should be curious about my older colleagues and get them to open up. Sounds like I might learn some good stuff if I do. But what about in the other direction? How can I get them to be more receptive to us young bucks and some of how we think about the future?"

"It doesn't matter who you are in conversation with; old, young, black, purple, or green. Everyone wants to be heard and treated with dignity. When we offer our ear and respect, we are more likely to get that in return."

All along I had been framing this culture transformation as old vs. new, analog vs. digital, backwards vs. forward. Sydney helped shift my perspective beyond binaries. I went back to Bailey and Charley. "What do you think would happen if we focused on storytelling instead of approaching this initiative as 'us vs. them'? The next time the EVP starts with the merger story, what if you said something like 'You return to that moment frequently. It must have significance to you. What is that?' Instead of pushing back, we can shift the conversation."

We all agreed to give this approach a try. We realized that if we really believed in diversity and inclusion, then we needed to make room for the whole spectrum of responses to organizational change. Otherwise, we didn't really believe in inclusion. By declaring These norms as good and Those as bad, many will feel left out and marginalized. This creates an "us vs. them" culture. Stories are a powerful way to create meaningful connections that break down those divisions. We found that when we listened deeply, we heard pride and that person's unique Voice. From this vantage point, people were more likely to hear *our* Voices. And sometimes we were surprised to experience a common bond that wasn't obvious before. These bonds formed a daisy chain of connections that added up to a collective effort to move forward with mutual respect. But this method didn't always work. There were arrogant assholes who thought we were sniveling idiots no matter how much respect we granted them. We didn't waste time on them. If our company was serious about this transformation, those people's bosses would deal with them.

This lesson gave me pause. I was such a smug shit thinking that I was The Role Model of the future and everyone else was a total loser stuck in the past. The company hired me to lead the way. I had a very judgmental view of anyone who saw things differently than I did. I was convinced that anyone who didn't hop on the train that had already left the station was useless to the organization. These conversations helped me to see the light. I was "that person." You know the one. The one you swear you are the exact opposite of. Self-righteousness can do that to you. I thought I was the fucking paragon of virtue and the future. Instead, I shut out other Voices as much as I accused others of doing.

THE BEST
LAID PLANS ...

My department oversaw the management of the main software platform the company used. Chris tasked me with upgrading the system. Working with Quinn had prepared me for such an analytic exercise, except I decided to approach the project as the anti-Quinn. I wasn't just going to do the math. I was going to find out what the staff and customers needed the system to do. I called it the Micah Method for Humanizing Corporate Initiatives.

Working with my best players, we moved through a detailed project plan. We assessed the current software and determined what was and wasn't working. We interviewed super-users to learn what they would like and grilled the vendor about all possible options to execute our goals. I kept Chris in the loop. Once we had a draft proposal, our team reviewed it with Chris, who raised some good questions and sent us back to tweak some issues. In the meantime, Chris gave the executive team a heads up. The execs signed off, and we commenced with implementing the project.

Chris made the formal announcement at an All Staff meeting. I made a bet with the team that the staff was going to piss and moan and throw tomatoes at Chris. I won a free lunch and Chris needed a dry cleaner. Initial shock and awe over, we commenced with enacting the game plan.

It was a fucking disaster. The customized modules had so many bugs that a whole can of Raid couldn't kill them. The modifications to the core part of the system were indecipherable. The customer service hotlines were burning up. The staff staged an open rebellion at vendor training sessions. On the bright side, I had negotiated that payment was contingent upon satisfaction.

Although Chris took a piece of the blame, I got the lion's share. My failure was not only as a result of missed steps in the planning, but also incomplete data gathering. I bounced between the angry mob, the incompetent vendor, my put-upon team and pissed off executives. Should I continue to work with the vendor to get things right? Should I scale things back? Should I junk the whole thing and convince the company to write down the loss? I was so far up shit's creek that I was forced to ask for help.

I felt humiliated and like the biggest fuckup. This was not a misstep visible only to my own team or department; it was company-wide *and* customer-facing. I felt exposed in such a raw way. Sydney tried to convince me that vulnerability and failure are great teachers. I told Sydney to fuck off. I prefer to be seen as always strong and in control. You know, like a superhero. Needing or asking for help made me feel weak. And yet, when I supervised or mentored, I always told people how it is a sign of strength to ask for help. What I meant, of course, was that it was fantastic if *they* asked for help but total shit if I did the same. After the initial shock wore off, I was less angry about needing help. I realized it wasn't the end of the world (or my career) and appreciated my colleagues' support. This was a new experience for me and it challenged me to grow in ways I discovered I needed to. It was another blow to my ego, which, until that disaster, I thought was in check. Oops.

So, I hit the pause button on all implementation activities to allow myself some time to figure out the best path forward. Next, I recruited a new small group to work with me. As a team, we explored what would happen if we wiped the slate clean, assessed our software requirements, and compiled a wish list? The initial responses differed from the input from my first team. I gave them two weeks to gather data, speak with more staff and customers, select critical priorities, and craft a strawman design. I told them to keep it simple and user friendly, otherwise I gave no other parameters.

After talking with Chris, I realized that I hadn't listened well enough. I was unconsciously pushing a cost cutting approach. Damn you, Quinn! I assumed that because I did ask for input that I had fully integrated what I heard. Instead, what I did was try to forcefit the feedback into a cost model. That's the asshole part. I took the "right actions" but didn't have the "right mindset."

I hired a consultant to plan and facilitate our day-long meeting to sort through the new information and to draw some conclusions. I didn't drive the discussion. In fact, if I tried to the consultant smacked me down. The consultant urged us to debate vigorously, advocate for strong positions, listen deeply, and look for places where we needed more information. It's amazing how productive high stakes conversations can be with outside facilitation. I was relieved of my duties to manage all the dynamics and opinions flying around the room. It was clear that this group had solicited more perspectives and had a more comprehensive view of the needs. We identified what data we still needed to gather and allowed ourselves more time to develop a plan.

We reconvened and integrated the new data. The consultant helped us identify the points of consensus and which divergent elements were important enough to incorporate. Ultimately, a solution emerged that was so much better than the initial plan. Rather than trot this by the senior leaders, we called in several premium customers and staff who were known critical thinkers. The consultant solicited candid feedback and then walked us through some real-time adjustments to the plan. By the end of the session, we had not just affirmation from this focus group, but genuine enthusiasm. What's even better was how simple the solution was.

We had three big issues to address: what to do about the vendor; how to fully implement the solution; and how to communicate to the staff. I could not afford to fuck up again. Chris joined me in renegotiating the terms with the vendor. We didn't want to junk the software, we just wanted to cut back on the extras we selected in the original plan. We insisted that Davi, from our new team, oversee the implementation and training. The vendor already proved their weak spot in training during the first go-round, and Davi could run circles around them. So, two problems solved.

Sydney helped me devise a communication strategy. I had to eat crow and regain the staff's trust before anyone would sign on to Plan 2.0. We cooked up a combination listening and explanation tour. Davi pulled together groups of 50 staff members around the company for us to meet with. At each session, I began with a sincere apology, then talked about what I had learned. "I screwed up and I know it will take time and good behavior before you trust me again. This whole mess made me sit myself down to figure out what went wrong and what is a better way forward. I thought I had taken all the right steps and listened to all the right people; I thought I had all the right analytics to come up with the right solution. Now I see that I had missed a few steps, didn't listen well enough, didn't have all the information, and had blinders on. As a result, I put out the wrong path forward. There were not enough voices in the mix and not enough debate. When we took a second pass at the possible solutions we used a different process that I think can serve as a model for future problem solving. We gathered together a more diverse working group, we used a consultant who required us to challenge the status quo and debate more vigorously, we learned how to set egos aside so we could truly hear what others were saying and we opted for thoroughness over expediency. That allowed us to come up with a unique plan that we believe is a much better one. This experience humbled me. Failure is a cruel and profound teacher. I hope that you will be receptive to the new plan and that you will help Davi implement it. Please ask for help along the way and we will do everything we can to create a success for all. Again, please accept my apology for causing so much confusion and stress."

While this was happening, I was certain that I had committed a Career Altering Moment. I felt like shit and hung my head as I walked around the building. These apology sessions were draining and sent me home to flop on the couch and pass out at the end of each day. I had no idea if this would work out or not but I was convinced that I was doing the right thing.

Bailey and Charley supported me along the way. They gave me pep talks and lots of chocolate as I tried to experience the thrill of victory rather than the agony of defeat. They reassured me that I would land on my feet. Chris's reaction confused me. On the one hand, they wanted me to accept full responsibility but on the other, they discouraged me from being so self-effacing with the staff. They preferred that I say something like, "Sorry about the mix up, I messed up and now here is what we are doing". They felt I diminished myself as a leader by being so vulnerable and worried the staff would begin to see me as weak.

The CEO's impression contrasted starkly with Chris's. We had a private conversation during my breast-beating tour. I, of course, figured this was curtains for me but I couldn't have been more wrong. They congratulated me on my courage and said that I exemplified the type of leadership they sought in the company. They wanted people to take full responsibility, make course corrections, bring in new voices and new methods, challenge everything, and take the risk of being more human in front of the staff. They hadn't seen many examples of that yet from anyone, including themself. They saw me as The Role Model of where the leadership team needed to go.

Hearing the CEO say this freaked me out. Of course, I loved the compliment and felt I had achieved my personal goals. But I neglected to factor in that with great power comes great responsibility. Being an example for others meant I had to think about everything I did and said. Fuck. Just the thought of that exhausted me. And what about my ego? It had just been deflated like a Patriots football only to be pumped up again. And what about my relationships with other leaders? I prayed that the CEO didn't put me on a pedestal with them. I had just fallen from ground level. I didn't want to develop a fear of heights.

Positive attention from the CEO worried me. Finding that balance between being a beloved standout leader and a despised one was new territory for me. This was a task for Sydney. With help, I kept my ego in check and lowered my anxiety and just went about the business of being the leader I was becoming. Wow. That sounded so new-agey. What I mean is that leadership doesn't happen all at once or in a straight line. There is a great deal of self-examination along the way that creates changed behaviors and new insights. In retrospect, this fuck up had a profoundly positive impact on my growth.

PASSING THE TORCH

Things sorted themselves out with the software project. Some bumps along the way but Davi handled them beautifully. I poured more energy into developing my team's top performers. I cooked up a cross-departmental project to increase their organizational visibility. It was a huge success and put both of them on the CEO's radar. I figured I was going to lose them to a bigger opportunity sooner than later, but understood that's the nature of the beast. Grow them and they will ultimately leave.

My peers hated the idea of investing in top people just to see them leave the organization. Call me cracked (and you'd have much company if you did), but I believe in just the opposite. If you *don't* grow your people, they will most certainly leave. And if you *do* develop them, they may stick around for continued opportunities and advancement right where they are. Or they may find better choices elsewhere. To this day, I just don't understand why so many leaders don't get this. Santana, once told me that a leader should be seen as a Talent Magnet. That image has stuck with me all these years.

At this point, my team was doing well, I had redeemed myself and my relationships with Chris and the CEO continued to evolve. I was doing a better job of juggling the triangulation between me, Chris and the CEO. And then I noticed tensions resurfacing between me and Chris. I wasn't sure what to make of it but it didn't seem troublesome enough to raise the topic. And then Chris asked me to go out for lunch away from the office. Shit.

White tablecloth and the end booth. A nice private spot for my lashing. Would it leave stains on the linens? I gulped my water and wished it was acceptable to order alcohol over a business lunch. Damn. How I wish I was back in the 80's.

Chris got to the point. "Micah, you've done some remarkable work over these past several years. I'm so pleased with your progress. And, frankly, I find myself brought up short. You are better than I am at leading and modeling this new culture. I hired you for all the right reasons and I now realize that I have some limitations in my own elasticity. You have surpassed me in both orientation and results."

I responded immediately. "Thank you for the feedback, but I think you sell yourself short. You must know that your leadership and supervision has allowed me to shine. You are the best boss I've ever had and I use what I've learned from you every day."

"That's kind of you. I hope that one of the things you've learned from me is to see yourself honestly. And to speak the truth. Here is the current reality, Micah. I'm on the ropes with the CEO. Although they think I've been a great performer all these years, I have stalled out. When they compare my habits to yours, I fall short. My worst fear is that they will push me out of here to make room for you."

I was nearly speechless. After several moments, I managed to speak. "This surprises me. I appreciate that you trust me enough to tell me. We could never be having this conversation without all those hours we have clocked building our connection. I don't know what to say."

"When I step back and look at the greater good of the company, I don't disagree with the CEO. I am a talented leader who doesn't fit as well with the new direction. And you are the future. Sometimes, the old guard needs to know when to move aside. Like most things, it isn't good to overstay your welcome because things can unravel. Although they haven't said it explicitly, I believe the CEO wants me to leave so you can take my slot but they are struggling with how to pull that off. I've thought this through and I want to be in charge of my own destiny. I'm still at the top of my game and highly marketable. I've been answering those calls from headhunters for several months and have explored a few options. My plan is to speak with the CEO about an exit strategy that gives me time to land well. In the meantime, we would agree to get you ready to take over my role. As I see it, everyone wins. I won't have to try to change and I will find a better role at a new company. The CEO won't have to fret about how to do the right thing, and you will get the well-deserved promotion."

This is what it looks like when a leader is selfless and serves the greater good. They had made significant contributions to the company over many years and, yet, this new culture direction revealed their limitations. Rather than do everything to hang on, Chris planned a graceful exit. They understood the need to give up seats at the table to bring in fresh perspectives. And they saw the CEO struggle with how to accomplish this with several other executives. Chris volunteered to help the CEO do the right thing.

Over the next several months, Chris and the CEO worked on the game plan. I was thrilled to have the chance to get additional coaching from Chris to prepare for my big move. This proved to be a compelling part of their narrative with the headhunters; how Chris invests in developing exceptional talent knowing that one day they may be replaced by them. Lots of leaders pay lip service to this but Chris really lived it.

No surprise, Chris landed extremely well. The CEO and I served as glowing references. I learned so much from Chris and continue to learn from them. We have stayed in close contact and our relationship has deepened.

It was now my turn to enter the inner sanctum behind the Big Double Doors. Despite the months of preparation, I felt like I was on the high wire without a net. I missed Chris something fierce.

AT THE
GROWN UPS'
TABLE

My initial excitement about the promotion quickly turned into frustration. I tried to wow my colleagues with my brilliance but they weren't having it. So then, I tried deference but it bordered on ass kissing. I tried to be the proud square peg but they lectured me about how things worked in their world. I tried sitting back and observing like a good student but they told me that I needed to assert myself. In short, there was no honeymoon period. To add insult to injury, I discovered there were no secret handshakes, fancy name plates or better coffee as a perk for being on the executive team. After too many nights of Marvel Avenger movies to ward off complete depression, I reached out to Chris for some advice.

"Why didn't you warn me?" I ranted. "I imagined meaningful discussions between smart colleagues committed to the success of the company. So far, all I see are weekly department updates where everyone insists that everything is going swimmingly and would go even better if other teammates would do their share. Silos, pettiness, tangents, and showboating. I busted my butt for *this*? And what about the CEO? It disappoints me that they aren't managing these personalities and agendas. It boggles my mind that they are so crappy at this executive team thing. Chris, you spoiled me for any new bosses. This is all your fault."

Chris laughed. "I'll take that compliment. And I understand what you're feeling. But, Micah, take a deep cleansing breath. In and out." This had become our little routine, this centering thing as a joke. I cracked a smile and gave the go-ahead nod.

"Even now, after I've left, I refuse to slam the CEO or my colleagues. If there is dirty laundry, good executives will deal with it privately. So, heed that advice. Here's the thing about an executive team that is different than other teams you have been on: it's a room full of people who are at the top of their game who earned those seats. Some may be more effective than others, some may be more decent than others but all of them got there for good reasons. Now they want to hold onto all the trappings of their success. Any time you gather a group of people with so much to lose, things will get weird. Defensiveness, chest beating, posturing. For the record, I wasn't my best self in that board room either."

"Terrific. Sounds like it's inevitable that I'll become an arrogant asshole too."

Chris paused. "Not inevitable, but you will need to resist the urge. My advice is for you to be courageous and just be the Micah that got you into that room. Don't let the mahogany change you. My other suggestion is to form individual relationships with each member. Take the time to learn about who they are and give them a chance to experience you separate from the team. That will help you feel at ease when everyone is together."

Ah, the old Chris trick. Form one-on-one connections with people to make the team experience more effective. I spent two months meeting off site with each of my colleagues to begin the process of building some connections.

ROBIN

Robin fancied themself as au courant but, in fact, was an impostor. When I asked them to, "Tell me a bit about yourself," they spent the next fifteen minutes regaling me with stories of their glory days. Career highs that were suspiciously absent of any lows. They had been with the company for some time and wondered why they hadn't ascended to CEO and made no effort to hide their resentment about that. It felt like the longest lunch of my life. So long.

At no point in our conversation did Robin mention any ideas about the future of the company, nor did they praise any other executive team members. And, lest I forget, they did not ask a single question about *me*. Fuck. Robin was a black hole for emotional intelligence; I felt perplexed as to whether they believed I found their behavior endearing or admirable. Were my boredom and disdain written all over my face?

Note to Self: I filed Robin under the "Don't Do That" list, the mental catalogue of professional types I had been keeping since the early days of my career. I wasn't so much worried about being like Robin, a huge asshole, as I was about being boastful. Humility is much more attractive.

CAM

Cam, on the other hand, was the exact opposite of Robin. Before my promotion, I admired them from afar and now I looked forward to learning more up close. Lo and behold, my lunch with Cam did not disappoint. They asked me a zillion questions about myself and

I don't remember them using the word "I" once. When they spoke of major initiatives they lead, they always gave props to the team. When I asked about pressing issues the company faced, they pointed me to a dozen people around the building we needed to tap to help solve the problems.

When I asked for guidance about how to assimilate into the executive team, Cam told me a story. "By the time I got to my current role, I had worked with most of the members of the team in other capacities. I arrived with an idea of their strengths and challenges and I had assumed that our prior connections would flow organically into our transition to working as peers. However, I found myself frustrated with a couple colleagues because I felt they weren't responding to me as an equal. The only thing that had changed was my title. I was still as competent and productive as ever and I expected that they would be as respectful and receptive as before. I was annoyed and wanted to confront the situation head on, but at the same time, I thought it might be better if I stepped back and observed for a bit. Ultimately, I stepped back and I'm glad that I did. What I learned was that this wasn't personal. They weren't disrespecting me, they were just caught up in the '*Dance of Status*'.

"Have you ever watched a group of kids on the playground? Some kids will pair up with a buddy while others will show off for the teacher. When a new child transfers into the class, everyone is wary. They worry, 'Will she become the teacher's pet?' or 'Will he become my best friend's new best friend?' It destabilizes the social order. That moment when a new person is introduced is awkward, especially for the new person. The '*Dance of Status*' goes into full swing and what happens next is most critical. The person who comes forward to be the new person's buddy is least interested in the drama. That person wants the group to succeed and is comfortable sharing the spotlight."

I had to ask. "So, who stepped forward to be *your* buddy?"

Cam wasn't biting. "If you sit back, your buddy will come to you. I appreciate my colleagues and have strong connections to all of them."

"Are you suggesting that I shouldn't try too hard initially and to let things unfold naturally? I need to trust that no one will leave me alone on the playground?"

"Exactly right. And in the meantime, don't take the slights personally. You earned your seat at the table and don't let anyone cause you to doubt that."

Note to Self: Even though I desperately wanted to be their new best friend, I also understood that they didn't play favorites. I knew we would evolve into a strong connection and I needed to resist my urge to rush things. Not my forte. Cam was added to the "Do This" list.

YAEL

My meeting with Yael blew me away. They were the classic visionary. There was no problem too complex or too big to solve. I knew about some high-profile projects they had worked on before they joined our company, so I asked them to tell me about it.

As with Cam, Yael demurred from lapping up praise for their accomplishments. "Oh, don't believe all the stories you hear. It really just boils down to an epiphany I had one day. Back when I was doing design work, I walked a mile through Manhattan to get to the office. Along the way, I passed dozens of homeless people. It made me wonder what was being done to solve this crisis and I spent months researching the topic. As I learned that they do not necessarily like going to shelters, I wondered how they stayed warm in the winter months. I thought to myself, 'Someone ought to solve this problem.' Then it occurred to me, 'why not me? *I* can figure out how to keep folks on the streets warm in the cold months.' So I designed outdoor heaters like the ones outside restaurants to be placed in locations around the city where homeless people gathered. I just feel grateful to have a small impact on the problem."

Yael never even mentioned the mayor's commendation, how other cities followed suit, or any of the publicity. Yael's eyes were on the prize, not the glory. Already impressed, I asked about their vision for our company.

"We have great products, great people, and great potential. I feel like we're holding back, playing it safe, so I hope that people like you will challenge the executive team to push beyond what is comfortable. That's my vision: that we will set our sights higher and do the unexpected. We need to talk more openly about what needs to be shaken up, what needs to be jettisoned and what needs to be invented. I believe that's what this whole culture change is meant to do."

Note to Self: Another ally. I was thrilled but also noted that Yael did not ask many questions, made some assumptions about my perspective, and was short on details. I wondered if they were an "idea-a-minute" person who wasn't much of a "doer". I wondered if they "had people" to take care of business on the ground. That's the thing about visionaries. You want to follow them because they passionately believe in the impossible but when the rubber hits the road, they are already on to the next cool idea. I imagined Yael as a fantastic sounding board but I wasn't sure about the rest.

BOBBIE

I had worked with Bobbie on a few projects in the past. Bobbie was brilliant, deeply understood our business, and was a huge asshole. When we met for lunch, they showed their true colors. "I can't fucking believe that everyone sheepishly sided with the CEO on the partnership agreement when there is no way that plan will fly. Cowards! This will be another I-told-you-so moment when this crashes and burns." Because we had history, I knew how to handle this. "Walk me through your thought process again."

I nodded, uttered loads of "hmms", leaned in, and kept asking questions for a full 45 minutes. Only when the server brought the check, did Bobbie finally say, "So, how are you liking the new job so far?" I was tempted to say something outrageous like, "Well, my first order of business will be to fire everyone and turn the building into an amusement park," because I knew they weren't actually listening to a word I said. Don't worry. I behaved.

Note to Self: The thing about Bobbie was that they were, in fact, smart, and they contributed to the business. But everything was about their intellectual superiority over others. Bobbie's M.O. was the four H's: harangue, harass, humiliate, and hurt. They aggressively believed in their "rightness". To their mind, unless a person agreed with them, they were an idiot and a nobody. But one could not express agreement through hero worship, because then Bobbie would label that person a sycophant who couldn't *truly* understand how brilliant they were, and they would respect them even less. Worst of all, Bobbie could turn all that aggression against an unsuspecting victim at a moment's notice. Up to this point, I had respected Bobbie when we had to interact, but generally kept them at arm's length. With my new spot on the executive team, I now needed to develop a real connection to them, but I wasn't sure how to get past all the bluster and arrogance to find the human being lurking inside.

PAT

Pat intimidated me, so I felt nervous before our lunch together. I knew they were a superstar but we didn't speak the same language. They spoke Tech and I spoke Human. I figured it was on me to become bilingual if we were going to have a good working relationship.

"Micah, I've been looking forward to this conversation all week. I only know you by reputation, and now I get to be one of your peers. Tell me about yourself and what you hope to accomplish in your new role."

Well, that was a surprise. Here was a big shot not acting like a big shot and they were speaking in my native tongue. I decided to pull back on the full-frontal Micah for now and just relax into an easy give and take. Good choice.

I told Pat about some ups and some downs and what I had learned along the way. They responded in kind. Before long, we were laughing about blunders we had made and anticipated the ones we were likely to make in the future. I was relieved to see this very accomplished person not take themself too seriously and I think they saw my capacity to do the same. Our time was over too quickly and we arranged an extended meeting for the following week. A spark was lit and we wanted more.

Note to Self: Up to this point in my career I had kept my distance from types like Pat. You know, geeks. My mind fogs, my senses numb and I struggle to stay awake. I rarely understand what they are saying and they don't seem to be interested in stuff I know. We are just different creatures. Total disconnect. But something cracked open for me with Pat. Now I realized that I screwed myself in the past by not getting to know these tech-types up close and personal. Maintaining that distance allowed me to stick with stereotypes I carried with me. Biases about who others were but also where my limitations were. If I believed I was a technical idiot, I was. I had also underestimated their interest in my expertise. Pat peppered our chat with questions and responded with "So, is it like this thing I know about?" and then we would go back and forth until we found shared language and experiences that formed a mutual understanding. Here I was, the "One Who Craves Differences", and I was totally shut down because of my own insecurities. So many missed opportunities for fun collaborations in my wake. My relationship with Pat turned out to be one I valued the most. We approached things from radically different places, challenged each other to get outside of our own brains, debated constantly, and always landed on solutions that were much cooler than either of us could have done alone. Meeting Pat was an "a-ha moment". It forced me to confront my own closed-mindedness and self-fulfilling prophecies. And this from the Diversity and Inclusion Champion! I can be so full of shit sometimes. So self-righteous. I needed to fix this.

TERRY

Terry was senior, but not in a good way. They had a fuzzy title that no one understood and seemed more like a potted plant in the corner than an active member of the executive team. What did they bring to the party? Not even a bag of chips, as it turns out. When we met, the conversation was disjointed and unintelligible. It was like a game of hunt and peck as I tried to figure out the puzzle that was Terry.

To start, I approached the conversation with deference. "You must have seen it all here. What do you think makes this place thrive?"

"Back in 1990, things were exciting. So many smart people, so many new things to pursue. That all ended by 2000. The last two decades have been shit. Idiots wandering the hallways and bigger idiots running the place."

Hoping to steer away from their negativity, I changed the subject. "Help me understand your current role. With such an impressive background, I'm sure you have a lot of insights to share."

"I'm an EVP because they couldn't figure out what else to do with me. I was so instrumental in our biggest successes that the board won't let me go. They count on me to keep an eye on the CEO."

Interesting. Could that be true? I tried again.

"What advice do you have for me as I step into this role?" People just love to be seen as the guru.

"Don't get too comfortable. You never know which way the wind will blow."

And with that, I gave up. I thanked them for their time and I'm fairly certain I saw them yawn as I left. What the fuck? Their salary alone could pay for four fantastic Directors. Why did the CEO allow Terry to take up space and resources? This tarnished my perception of the CEO.

Note to Self: If I was upset with the CEO for keeping Terry, I assumed the staff was too. I remember sitting in the cheap seats and wondering why some Do Nothing was sitting in the front row. Tenure or ancient successes didn't seem like a good enough reason. My peers mostly ignored Terry, which would be easy for me to do. But my disappointment (again) with the CEO was another matter.

DANA

I had many occasions to work with Dana before my ascent and none of them were my idea of a good time. Everyone knew that their team had the highest turnover of any department in the company. As a result, I dragged my feet before meeting with Dana.

They remained behind their desk when I walked into their office. I remembered a tidbit from my HiPo training course. The instructor explained that staying at your desk and not removing the distance between you and the person you were meeting with was *the* classic power move. And here I was, just where Dana wanted me.

"Welcome aboard, Micah. It was good of you to schedule this meeting. I'm sure you have many questions that I'm happy to answer for you."

I decided not to fight and played my part as the good, obedient supplicant. "Thanks for taking the time. I wonder if you could share your thoughts about how I can be an effective member of our team."

"First of all, remember that we've all been at this much longer than you have. Sit back and learn. If you want to get ahead around here you need to respect the hierarchy."

I thought I could beat them at their own game, but their condescension struck my ego and I just couldn't hold back. "Okay. But I hope there is room for us to collaborate as equals."

Dana leaned over their desk and glared at me. "You know, I heard you were an upstart. Someone who prides themselves on their 'people skills'. That may have worked for you before but on this team, we value two things: results and respect for authority."

"Are you telling me that the executive team members are supposed to line up behind the CEO and then in order of tenure to be valued?"

"You really are naïve, just like the rest of your generation. You have no concept of the value of experience and expertise. To you, everything is a conversation or rah-rah team or fresh new idea. That's wasted time when we need to achieve our goals. There will be no Participation Trophies given out on this team. Bring the results and you will gain some respect."

And so it went. Dana's rigidity, dictatorial posture and hostility all registered as fear to me. Rather than feeling repelled by them, I felt sorry for Dana. They seemed terrified of being displaced by the new and young wave in the company. Although I didn't have any ideas about how, when I walked out of their office I vowed that I would find a way to crack through their hard shell. Inside, I knew there was a smart, accomplished human being in need of a deep, deep tissue massage.

Note to Self: Talking with Dana also reminded me that the generational divide is a real thing. Young people view older folks as past their prime while the veterans see their younger peers as inexperienced rookies with unwarranted self-confidence. So much finger-pointing and criticizing eliminates any possibility of learning from each other and combining forces. Young people don't need to feel threatened by a wealth of experience and older people don't need to freak out about all that new-fangled thinking.

JULES

I was excited to establish a close working relationship with Jules because I had heard both high praise for their inventive results on the one hand, and criticisms about their personal style on the other. It raised several questions in my mind, "Does substance win over style? Do you need both? If you had to choose, which is a better leadership strategy?"

We met for lunch at an off-the-beaten-track bistro. I hadn't been to this place before and I said so. Jules said, "Neither have I. I thought we would give it a try." Turns out, we were both foodies and that formed an easy and quick bond.

In between bites, we introduced ourselves. Unlike my other peers, Jules told me where they grew up, something about their family story, college years, previous jobs and why they came to this company. I returned the favor. It was a more personal conversation that put me at ease and made me even more interested in developing this relationship. By the time we were talking about the executive team and what was happening with the company, Jules already felt like an old friend.

"Jules, I'm interested to know what you think our team needs to focus on."

"That's a great question that I wish I could answer simply. I have strong opinions about what we need to do and I'm not shy about expressing them. But I don't feel the team is willing or able to have a conversation about big ideas. I worry that some opportunities will pass by us if we don't take action soon, but the CEO and our colleagues don't share my perspective. I feel like I'm the kid running around the room saying the house is on fire while everyone else sits and stares. At this point, I don't care if they agree with my ideas. I'd be happy just to open up the debate."

"That's disappointing to hear. But I've been meeting with everyone individually on our team, and I think there are some like-minded folks in the bunch, don't you?"

"There are. Maybe your presence will tip the balance. That would be great. I'm getting tired of sending up a flare, getting shot down, and then going back to my own department and doing what I think is best. Not exactly ideal."

"No, it's not. If you don't mind me asking, how do you deal with your frustration?"

Jules laughed. "Not too well, I'm afraid. Ask anyone. I have a reputation for being rather grumpy. But I'm not actually grumpy. I'm passionate about what we do here and I want us to stay ahead of the curve. I don't always express myself calmly or tuck away my displeasure. But don't draw the conclusion that I'm a jerk."

I realized I was wondering about the wrong stuff; substance vs. style. Where did I get that crap? Sounds like some MBA bullshit. One thing I knew for sure, I wanted to spend as much time with Jules as possible. We made a pact that day that I was always welcome at any of their meetings and to poke around their department as I pleased. I came to call that corner of the organization my Learning Lab. And on my bad days, I would seek refuge there and renamed it My Happy Place.

Note to Self: Jules challenged my ordinary way of thinking. My relationship with them helped me realize that I didn't know shit about how to be a multi-dimensional person in such a visible role. I had stayed true to myself but Jules made me see that I was a long way from showing up with my whole self. I was still playing it safe, fitting into a mold of my own creation. Because I was such a hot shot superhero, I had (falsely) assumed that I had come into my fullness of being. That this square peg had remained so. I call bullshit! Some of my edges had been ground down, my ego was still more pesky than I wanted and I wasn't staying focused on the big picture. I desperately needed Jules' tutorial because it sure as shit wasn't going to happen on the executive team. I wanted to follow their example without being too much of a groupie. Fortunately, we established a habit of periodic restaurant excursions to try new places. It was over those meals that I found a trustworthy peer where I could speak my mind. And that was before the bottle of wine.

That was the cast of characters on the executive team. Chris, as usual, was right. Establishing individual relationships with my peers was the right foot to start on. It helped me understand some of the confusing interactions that pinged around the room during our meetings. And it gave me food for thought as I evolved.

THE CEO,
UP CLOSE

I both hoped and expected that my past encounters with the CEO foreshadowed the wonderful things that lay ahead. Unfortunately, expectations are the shortest path to disappointment.

The CEO came up through West Point and went on to become an engineer. As a result, they were methodical, analytical, ethical, and team oriented. All good stuff. They were weaker when it came to anything involving variation, flexibility, creativity, conflict, or chaos. They visibly struggled to allow for subversive behavior. You know, like the stuff I'm tempted to do. There was this one time they pulled me aside after a meeting where I had been particularly provocative, urging the team to think more boldly. "Micah, I'm trying to get more comfortable with people like you but I just don't think I can change my stripes." Props for being that self-aware. It was a start.

One up-side of someone wired like the CEO is their moral clarity. For instance, a VP confided in me that she was being stalked and harassed by another VP. It was so severe that she was being treated for panic attacks and having people escort her to her car each night. She was a superstar on the rise while her peer was running a new and important business venture. At first, she begged me not to tell anyone because she worried about how it would reflect on her. I persuaded her to let me discuss this with the CEO on her behalf.

I closed the CEO's door. "I have a sensitive matter to share with you. I'm coming to you because of the exposure and the people involved." They listened as I described this woman's last six months of terror. When I finished, they immediately called the head of HR. "I want you to fire this VP today and have him permanently removed from the building."

I was stunned. "Aren't you going to do a formal investigation? He might try to sue. Also, he's in charge of a huge book of business. Are you just trusting the other VP?"

"I won't have this type of behavior in our company. I know this VP and I trust her completely. I also know the other VP and I find the accusations credible. Let him try to sue. I expect anyone at the senior level to be beyond reproach. Period."

In that moment I realized how far a good leader should go to do what's right. Regardless of the subsequent legal hoops and political fallout, the CEO didn't hesitate to call out and punish inappropriate or destructive behavior. At the time, I thought the CEO was being courageous. Now, I think they were just doing the right thing.

For better or for worse, the CEO also felt ferocious loyalty to their team. Despite knowing that some senior people had passed their "use by" dates, the CEO refused to toss them out. Terry, Robin and Dana had jobs for life. Chris told me that when they volunteered to step aside, the CEO worried about Chris's family. Only after Chris reassured them that everything was fine, did the CEO relax. While loyalty and concern for others' well-being are admirable traits for a leader, it can't come at the expense of the collective. Isn't finding that balance one of the reasons CEOs get paid the big bucks? I put this in the "Further Study Required" category.

The CEO was an effective communicator in front of the troops, set the vision for the future, was accessible to all, and understood that change takes persistent commitment. At the same time, they had visible weaknesses in leading the company's cultural transformation. They struggled to embody new behaviors and to restructure the executive team in a meaningful way.

These disappointments in leadership were nothing new to me, but as a member of the executive team, I now had a seat at the table and an opportunity to actually do something about it. How could I step up and do the right thing without some of my peers or even the CEO fully on board? This required time on Sydney's couch.

"So, here's the deal, Sydney. The CEO has so many good qualities and I do trust they are steering the company in the right direction. It's just that we could be doing so much better and more cutting edge stuff if they shook things up a bit. For one, they need to get more serious about this culture transformation. All inspiring talk, not enough action. And secondly, they need to do something about the executive team. Change out some people, facilitate discussions about important things rather than operational updates, get us to model the change we are asking the staff to embody. I feel like the overall plan looks good on paper but the drawings are sitting on a shelf somewhere gathering dust. Is the CEO really serious about making changes? When I was younger I was captivated by pretty words. Now I know better. Actions do speak louder than words and I can't understand why the CEO, or any leader for that matter, doesn't get that?"

Deep cleansing breath.

Sydney chuckled. "So you're looking for a perfect leader?"

"Of course, I am! Why should I settle for less?"

"No leader, including yourself, is great at *everything*. We wish for unrealistically perfect leaders because we imagine that will soothe our anxieties. A super-human will make sure that everything is alright, that everything turns out great. Aware of this expectation, leaders play along and pretend to have Superpowers. Leaders and staff who buy this fairy tale will be disappointed or angry. If a leader can't be human and if others around them can't accept that, the situation will be untenable."

Okay. I knew this already. But I needed the reminder. I wanted the CEO to be an impossible ideal of a self-actualized leader so that my life would be easier. I wanted them to change our team so I wasn't so frustrated. I wanted them to speed up this transformation so I had more compadres. I want. I want. I want.

Sydney offered an alternative. "What would happen if you accepted the CEO just as they are right now? If they never changed one ounce? Would you view them as an effective leader?"

"I would still consider them one of the better leaders I have encountered, and I would model some of my own behavior based on their example."

How many more years would it take me to let go of this superhero idea of leadership? Hadn't I gotten my own ass kicked enough times for believing I had Superpowers? How could I judge others for being imperfect? Another shitty part of me that needed to be cleaned up.

Before I left, Sydney offered once last gem. "Carl Jung established a whole branch of psychology that I find especially helpful in understanding ourselves and others. He wrote, "Everything that irritates us about others can lead us to an understanding of ourselves." I suggest that when you react strongly to the CEO or others on the team that you ask yourself where that trait shows up in yourself. You might manage your frustrations better. Not to mention that it could turn on your compassion switch instead."

What a lucky bastard I am to have found Sydney.

MOVING RIGHT ALONG

By the time I was in my role for eight months, I had the lay of the land. I decided to take a more generous perspective about the CEO and was bonding well with some of my peers. Pat, Jules, Cam and I joined forces to push our departments to be more inventive and integrated. We formed cross-functional teams to focus on new product development, streamlined processes and created closer customer relationships. By combining the talent and effort, we were living the principles of the culture transformation. We hit fast forward and our people couldn't have been more engaged and productive. We decided that, collectively, we owned a huge part of the business and we didn't need to mirror the CEO and other laggards. I was a pig in shit.

I hung out with Yael frequently to observe and learn how to think much bigger than my usual habits. I took those lessons back to my own team with some success. I discovered that being a visionary is hard wired; not easily learned and implemented. Sure, I could connect some seemingly disconnected dots to create a new thought path. But Yael could make 2+2=world peace. I accepted their exceptional gift and my limitations but still pressed myself to keep trying.

The situation with Bobbie had lots of red flashing warning lights. Even though our direct contact was infrequent, they seemed to find fault every time I opened my mouth in our executive team meetings. My ideas were dismissed, my results were debated and my conversations with others were interrupted. Their scowls and nasty tone were on full display. I noticed others getting some of this shit from time to time but for me it was a steady diet. They made their disdain for me vocal and visible.

I got supportive guidance from my peers. I learned that Bobbie always found an object of their scorn and that it was my turn. The past recipients of this great honor were people of the same gender who threatened their status in the food chain. If I entered the ring to do battle, I would lose. Not because others weren't good fighters but because the CEO never brought down the hammer on Bobbie. They advised me to ignore as much as possible, don't take the bait and see if the CEO finally does something about this. Great. There's always someone to spoil the party.

One year into my tenure, the CEO scheduled an executive team offsite to focus on innovation. I smelled disaster. How could we talk about creativity and collaboration and challenging the status quo if we couldn't even talk about the ordinary stuff? "Team" felt like the wrong word to describe my peer group; teams require trust and respect as a baseline, and we had not gotten there. I knew that no one felt comfortable enough to speak their mind or openly debate important issues. What was the CEO thinking? Doomed before we began.

A consultant designed and facilitated the meeting, but to my dismay, the outside intervention didn't lead to a magical breakthrough. The consultant planned the agenda well, stated clear objectives and gave pointed feedback. Despite their best efforts, the conversations were safe without many new ideas emerging. Even when My Posse suggested some cool stuff, nothing caught fire. Everyone looked to the CEO for hints at how to respond, and a very classic hub and spoke dynamic persisted. So, with or without outside help or fun topics, the team stayed stuck.

The consultant, clearly frustrated, offered feedback to the team and the CEO during the last twenty minutes of the day. "It seems we did not achieve the goals for the day. That's a shame since there is so much talent sitting here. I observed a tremendous reluctance or inability to engage in meaningful dialogue as a team. Whether that is from old patterns, fear, discomfort or unspoken conflict, I couldn't say. But I do know that teams need to develop muscles to interact productively to take an organization to the next level. If you continue to defer to the CEO and avoid healthy debates, you will remain constricted as a team and as a company. Can anyone explain why it is so difficult to have a stimulating conversation?"

Dead silence. Trust me, I was not going to say what was on my mind. Suicide isn't my thing. I hoped that Cam would say something. They have a way of speaking the truth in ways that are helpful rather than harmful. Aware that I lacked that skill, I kept quiet. Finally, the CEO ended the tension. "Maybe the problem is me. Maybe I don't step back enough, and you don't feel like you can challenge me."

Again, dead silence. But I was pleased with the CEO's vulnerability and trying to figure out how to support them. Cam beat me to the punch. "I appreciate your candor. I can only speak for myself but I feel completely comfortable talking about anything with you when it is one-on-one. But I don't feel that way when the team is gathered. And, because it is a team, I would say we are all responsible for what takes place." Several of us chimed in with similar observations. But half the team remained silent.

The consultant tried to use the opening but it went nowhere. This group was deeply entrenched in old habits and extremely mistrustful. We left the session without moving forward in a meaningful way. In fact, the dinner that followed was a waste of good liquor and fine food. I did not rush to work the next morning. I felt drained and exhausted.

A week later the CEO scheduled an hour-long meeting with me. I wasn't sure if I should be worried. Mostly, I was curious. They began the conversation by asking me what I thought of the offsite meeting. I gave some innocuous answer but they pressed me to be more honest. I took a page from Cam's playbook and said, "As the newest member who is still observing and learning, I do notice that your voice and presence looms large when the team is together. Everyone seems to gauge what they are going to say based on where they think you are. Have you noticed this yourself?"

"Yes, I have but I can't seem to change this after all this time. I know that I control the room and that the team respects me. But that shouldn't shut down conversation. It frustrates me that I can't spur on a more robust debate."

"Trust me, you're not the only one who is frustrated. I agree with you that some of it is having the unique role and power of being the CEO. But there are nine other people in the room also contributing to the dynamic."

And then, the nugget. They tell me, "I feel so tense during our meetings that I just dread them. I fantasize about cancelling them most weeks." The CEO's vulnerability and addressing an issue so directly provided an opportunity for me to have an impact. "Don't blow it" I told myself.

I visualized Cam as I finally responded. "Can you tell me more about that dread?" Create a dialogue, not a monologue. Make a connection.

"It takes many forms," they began. "Sometimes, it's about the players in the room. Are these the right people? Do I need to make changes? What will the impact of those changes be? Sometimes, it's about the poor quality of the conversation. It seems that no matter what the topic is, everyone's responses are predictable. Most of the time, I just feel that I'm not doing a very good job managing the personalities, the dynamics or the discussion. That I'm stuck in my own bad habits. I've reached out to you and a couple other team members to have a more candid conversation about how to fix this."

I was so drawn into their self-disclosure that my ego stayed (thankfully) tucked away. It was easy for me to reply. "I'm certain that long before this role, you struggled with building the right team. We all have. And I think we would agree that teams are extremely challenging. You are not alone or even unique in your frustrations, and this is solvable. I'm wondering if you have considered getting a coach?"

The CEO chuckled and said, "Well, that makes it a consensus! Everyone seems to be offering the same guidance. If I remember correctly, you have a coach, right? I've never had one and I wonder if you can tell me something about that."

I decided to return the favor of self-disclosure and shared a couple examples of times that Sydney had set me on the right path with my team. I described my errors, my difficulties in focusing inward instead of outward and specific suggestions that Sydney made me try. I told them that one size does not fit all and that trying new things while maintaining my truest sense of self is scary *and* exciting. I made sure not to prattle on too long or gush too much. The CEO was more reserved than I was and I didn't want to overwhelm them.

"Micah, this is very helpful. I've engaged coaches for so many of my direct reports over the years but somehow thought I didn't need help. I guess I've reached my limit and want to learn some new tricks. I know that I don't want to keep hitting my head against the wall."

And just like that, we cemented our relationship. It wasn't about some fantastic initiative I led or being the new kid on the block. We simply made a human connection. Setting the roles aside, letting the masks fall away, revealing painful and hopeful truths. I vowed to embrace this approach in my future interactions.

The CEO hired the consultant who had worked with our team to individually coach them and occasionally work with the whole team. It was a year of tremendous shifting. The CEO emerged as a person who listened more, asked more questions, drew out others and made more meaningful connections with each direct report. The team loosened up and challenged the CEO and others on their thinking. There were fewer predictable agreements and more debate. We weren't always productive but at least we were talking to each other instead of posturing. Sparks flew between members as we collaborated and coordinated more with each other. Less isolation and more esprit de corps.

It wasn't perfect but at least we were moving in the right direction. The CEO had more pep in their step and the business results were improving. There were still some questionable people on the team and I was curious to see how long it would take before the CEO addressed those issues. With the changes, the stinkers were more obvious. They weren't too thrilled about where things were going and it was harder for them to hide or keep pulling the same old shit.

Deep cleansing breath.

HOW TO TRAIN
EX-PEERS

I kept Sydney's lesson about the myth of the "perfect leader" top of mind as I focused on my own team. In the unusual position of transitioning from their peer to their supervisor, I anticipated the pitfalls in making the shift. That didn't stop me from going a bit nutty. Rather than descend into my own insanity, I decided that our team offsite had to set the tone for this new relationship.

My team consisted of supercharged experts at the top of their games. They bought into the culture transformation even though they struggled to make some adjustments to their own habits. There was ego aplenty and competition that bordered on aggression. Since I already had one-on-one relationships with everyone, I had a better working knowledge of this cast of characters than with previous teams. And they knew me so I could cut to the chase more quickly at our retreat.

When the team walked into the meeting room, they had a gorgeous view of the woods outside the wall of windows. There were comfy chairs arranged in a circle and Miles Davis music set the mood. Coffee and breakfast were set up in the corner and everyone mingled and ate until it was time to gather in the circle.

"Many of you know that I led a significant 'go green' initiative at my last company. It was one of those tasks where I had to use persuasion to get anything done. It's no secret that I can be a pushy character, especially when I'm passionate about something. To say that I was greeted with resistance and skepticism by my colleagues is being polite. One person even screamed in my face. I was so frustrated that I went to see the CEO, who was the sponsor for this effort. They listened patiently as I described the brick walls I was hitting but wasn't particularly sympathetic or helpful. I was wondering if they were serious about this project. And just like that, I had a fit with the CEO. My fists were balled up, my anger surfaced and I began to rant. I don't recall my words but I do remember the feelings and the look on the CEO's face. I had their attention and the veil dropped. They acknowledged the staff resistance and my emotions. I was trying to calm down when suddenly the CEO burst into their own rant. The distance between us faded and we were two impassioned people who were pissed off. Needless to say, this was not our usual behavior. I left the meeting with mixed feelings. I was glad there was a breakthrough but I was also worried that the CEO would think I was a zealot. And not the good kind. At the next staff meeting, the CEO made a thoughtful but aggressive plea to everyone about the value of this green initiative. They made it clear there would be consequences for not cooperating. I was shocked.

"The most important thing I learned from this incident is that showing emotions, being vulnerable, not sugar coating the truth is a powerful way to connect with others. Even a CEO. I was so worried that being that spontaneously real would be a Career Altering Moment. But just the opposite happened. It enhanced my standing.

"I have come to celebrate my inability to routinely tuck away huge parts of my personality. It is mostly useful, sometimes disarming and seldom horrible. When I was younger, being so intense or expressive made me feel odd and different. Now, I see it as an asset. I've learned how to manage it so I don't get into trouble. And honestly, I probably tamp it down more than I ought to. A work in progress. Today, I'd like us to learn about unique traits that are less known to each other. Something about yourself that has made you feel like an odd duck or that you didn't fit in. Maybe something that you, too, believe gives you an advantage. Tell your story."

My tale exposed my vulnerability and opened up the team dialogue. I was hoping to recreate that spontaneous sharing that occurred at one of my first team offsites at my previous company. It's always a gamble to try to orchestrate a magical moment. But my team jumped in whole-heartedly. Phew! We heard stories of being the only...gay person, non-Christian, non-white. We learned about coping strategies for dyslexia, overcoming stage fright, chronic excessive helping, video game obsession. Each tale was filled with anguish and triumph, embarrassment and pride. At the end of three hours this team, that had known each other for several years, discovered the depth of human development and untapped resources. It was like an infusion of new energy and new connections.

The new bonding set the stage for my afternoon plans. My goal was to get this collection of race horses to tone down their competitive power grabs. I began the next conversation this way. "Not surprisingly, with all this talent and achievement there is some unproductive competition. It surfaces in different ways. I have observed people being shot down, aggressive or self-righteous arguments, sabotage of other people's work, lack of collaboration and ego boosting declarations. I'd like our team to grow past all this. I know what fuels my less attractive competitive fires and I'd like to hear what it is for you.

"For me, I'm afraid of sounding stupid. No matter what credentials I have accumulated over the years, I still worry sometimes that I won't be perceived as smart enough. I don't know about you, but when I was growing up our dinner table was open warfare. We were competing for our highly knowledgeable father's approval. News of the day, complex vocabulary in several languages, politics, culture, human nature. You name it. My siblings and I went so far as to prep for mealtimes. Can you imagine that? It was enough to give me indigestion. By the time I was in my 20's, I saw it for what it was; a game. Unfortunately, the world of work makes me feel all the same things I did as a ten-year-old. Not as smart as my siblings, not enough to capture my father's attention. Trust me, I've worked to tame this beast with some success. But I'm sure you've noticed my competitive peccadillos. Steely cold tone, adamant, defensive, don't-even-think-of-challenging-me. I know it's not pretty and I know it shuts down all rational conversation. I'll need your help to keep growing."

This opening hit a nerve. I watched people shut down and fold into themselves. Revealing the underbelly of their competitive natures was asking a lot. So, I waited. I let the silence hang out there. Minutes passed as everyone stared at the woods or their shoes. Finally, one member spoke up.

"I can relate to what you said, Micah. One of my siblings is a neurosurgeon and the other is a Rhodes Scholar. I'm the under-achiever in the group and gave up trying to compete with them long ago. I've tried to carve out my own path but my insecurities follow me everywhere. I attempt to ignore them or push them away. But I think what happens instead is that I aim to prove that I'm the smartest person in the room by being an asshole. It's never my intention to disrespect anyone. But I know that's how I come off."

The ice was broken and everyone took the risk to expose their most unflattering traits. Not everyone had a ton of insight and almost no one had a clue about how to curb their fears. But the pattern was clear. Everyone suffered from self-doubt, fear or insecurity. The competitive behaviors that emerged from those feelings ranged from passive-aggressive to combative to dominance to isolation. One fascinating dynamic I observed was that there was no cross-talk like in the morning session. No one probed for more detail or offered feedback. Everyone just spoke in turn without any dialogue. I needed to get us back to a give and take.

"I appreciate that each of you took the risk to speak up. I know this wasn't easy. It would be more comfortable to see each other in the best possible light. But we are all just fully human which means that we have a dark side. I believe that when we don't fess up to our less flattering traits, it becomes very easy to get away with misbehaving. I also believe our team can do remarkable things but this internal competition will limit us. Now that we know more about the hidden worries that prompt this unproductive battle, I'd like us to problem solve about how we can collectively manage these dynamics. How can we build connection and empathy and minimize the tensions?"

Again, there was silence and empty stares. We were in high risk, un-familiar territory. No one talks about troublesome personality quirks and insecurities at work. While I waited (less patiently) for someone to speak up, my own inner dialogue went nuts. What the fuck was I thinking? This is way too touchy-feely for a team meeting. I blew my big chance to show how I was going to lead differently. Now they'll think I'm a complete screw up. And just as I was reaching peak des-peration, one brave member took the reins.

"Micah, as you can see, we are all so uncomfortable with this topic. But as I have been sitting here listening to everyone and reflecting on my own crap, a thought occurred to me. Maybe this is exactly what we need. Each of us, in our own right, has excelled. As a team, we have done some great things but, if we are honest, we would admit there is a wall we hit frequently that causes us to scatter and separate from each other. I think you are onto something by having us focus on unhealthy ways we compete with each other. I, for one, know when I do it but I never stopped to think about why. I'm sitting here realizing I need to figure that out. Not just for the sake of the team. But for my own leadership aspirations."

"I'm ready to jump out of my skin talking about this stuff. Which makes me realize that it must be important."

"We sure give a lot of lip service to how change makes people un-comfortable. By people, we mean other people. Not us. Maybe this team is a safe enough place to be uneasy."

Not everyone joined in whole-heartedly but eventually everyone agreed that one-upmanship was destructive to the team. As the conversation continued, I could hear the empathy and compassion override the anxieties. A consensus arose around how to shift gears. If someone is made to feel less than, they throw a yellow flag on the play. Literally. Then the conversation stops, a back and forth between the two parties ensues, a course correction is made and then it's back to work. There was also a strong sentiment that everyone had to do their own personal work to develop insight and new habits around the urge to triumph over others. We did not need to do group therapy. We just needed to deal with our own shit.

The rest of the day was more playful. They had done a lot of hard work and they needed a good reward. I'll be honest. I wasn't sure what would happen after this meeting. It was clear that I, too, was going to have to be uncomfortable and take that leap of faith. Part of me was curious and excited. The other part was terrified.

At this point, I knew that when we truly see another person in all their complexity and human being-ness, it is harder to mistreat them. It is harder to stereotype them, it is harder to dismiss them, it is harder to make assumptions about them. If we understand a person, when we see them act like an asshole it is harder to write them off. We are more likely to ask them what is going on. When we reveal more bits of ourselves with the people we work with, it is possible to make a meaningful connection. And those connections make it possible to do more incredible work together.

I knew this to be true because I saw it up close some years ago at my last job. There was a particularly brilliant but introverted EVP. People always described them as remote, inaccessible, aloof and disconnected. And the EVP wondered why no one knocked on their door or talked to them in the hallways. Then there were a series of town hall meetings where each EVP was interviewed. When it was this person's turn, someone asked why they were always locked away in their office. With a quiver in their voice they responded, "I'm painfully shy and awkward. Always have been. I know I should be roaming about and making myself more visible. But it is nearly paralyzing for me." The staff was so surprised that many people offered kind words and invited them to just try to show up more. I could see them smile and lighten up a bit. Finally, they offered, "Okay. I have a request of all of you. I will make more effort to come out of my office. So, when you see me all dazed and confused wandering the halls, please come up and talk to me. Don't leave me standing alone! I wouldn't be able to bear it." They got a standing ovation at that point. From that day forward, the EVP forced themselves to resist the urge to retreat and the staff was warmly generous. There were connections made and old labels fell away.

I hoped for similar experiences to occur on my team. But I wasn't sure that I, or my team, had the same courage as that EVP. I was more Cowardly Lion than one of the Avengers.

GETTING RID OF
THE ASSHOLE

The CEO's evolution resonated throughout the organization. At all levels, employees pushed for richer, deeper, riskier discussions, which led to major decisions. The aggressive assholes who were used to getting their way didn't take kindly to the company's new direction.

Parker, the one shithead on my direct report team, never missed an opportunity to assert their opinion, hit people over the head with it, demean anyone who challenged them, and huff with righteous indignation if the collective overruled them. I tried to supervise and coach them to reform without luck. I issued warnings, wrote frank performance reviews, and made my expectations crystal clear. Nothing changed.

I had experience firing people, but Parker was combative and potentially litigious. So when the time came to do the deed, I had my ducks in a row: written documentation over an extended period of time, legal guidance and sign-off, written harassment complaints from staff and HR presence during the exit conversation.

When Parker walked into my office and saw the HR person, they had no doubt about what was going down. True to form, they took the first shot before I had the chance. "You can't fire me. I own a significant piece of our revenue and the CEO has my back."

I was ready. "Sit down, Parker. Over the past ten months we have had repeated discussions about your unproductive and disruptive behavior. You have had multiple opportunities and resources to make changes but you haven't budged. In fact, you flat out refused and dismissed my objections as unwarranted. You apparently have no intention of improving so we are severing our relationship with you, effective immediately."

Next came Parker's snarky and threatening remarks. I cut them off, asked for their ID badge, and instructed the HR person to follow them to their work station to gather their belongings. Parker was unmoved. As in, did not move from the chair. Instead, they pulled out their cell phone and called the CEO, and I called in the security guard. The CEO answered Parker's call just as the guard entered my office. We all waited and tried not to smile.

Parker bemoaned to the CEO the injustice of being fired. As they listened to the CEO's reply, they turned white. Beads of sweat formed on their face and turned into little rivers of tears down their cheeks. Reality set in over their face. The security guard and HR escorted Parker out of my office and that was the last I heard from them.

The moral of the story is Choreography. When you need to get rid of a troublemaker, never go it alone. Call in all the appropriate resources and anticipate what threats they will make. Don't be shy about asking the big guns to back you up. The thing about assholes is they delude themselves to believe they are untouchable. That somehow the rules don't apply to them. That they are too valuable to the business to be fired.

Every week that passed without taking out Parker caused pain to my people and fed Parker's delusion of invincibility. I made every excuse in the book to avoid the inevitable. "The business will suffer! It will be too disruptive! Institutional knowledge I can't replace! They'll go to the competition!" All bullshit.

Eventually I realized that the drama surrounding the ordeal was not about Parker; it was about me. My people wondered what happened to my spine and assumed I was intimidated. Why did I allow this shithead to cause so much damage? They lost confidence in me and I heard whispers about some of them looking for the exit door. What the fuck was wrong with me? Was I intimidated?

I had a critical conversation with Sydney about this. "Micah, what are you afraid of?"

Me, afraid? No way! But once my defenses fell away, I fessed up. "I'm afraid to admit that I blew it right out of the chute. I saw Parker for who they were and I didn't nip it in the bud. Parker and people like Parker are not just bullies, they're pathological. Not completely of sound mind, but with a dash of genius thrown in. Parker is a lone wolf who doesn't play well with others. They want to dominate and get results on their own. I should have dealt with them a long time ago, and the longer I avoided it, the worse the dynamic became. It looked like Parker won and I lost, so I just felt stuck."

Sydney reassured me that most humans respond to people like Parker the way I did. They also said that it is never too late to say no. Sydney helped me swallow my pride and embarrassment and tuck my ego into bed. I didn't need help with the action plan. I needed help with my disappointment with myself.

Here's the big a-ha for me. Avoidance is the canary in the coal mine. I knew there was bad shit ahead but my ego made me ignore the situation. My gut was screaming "take the bull by the horns" but I didn't have the courage to act. I now pay close attention to that disconnect between what I know is right and what I do. While I allowed Parker to act out, I nearly lost some great team members. I'm pleased to report that there were some great discussions within our team minus Parker and I have never allowed another Parker to darken my door since.

EXECUTIVE
DIS-ORDERS

While I was wrestling my own demons, the CEO finally whooped some ass of their own. I'm guessing that they had conversations with their coach about some of the less than stellar members on the executive team. Terry "retired early to spend time with their family" and Robin changed from insubordinate to obsequious. Dana seemed to loosen up, so I decided to see if I could make a connection.

A project that I was heading had hit a few rough patches, so I decided to approach Dana for help, with the ulterior motive to weasel my way into their good graces. I invited Dana to my office for our meeting and was sitting at my round table when they entered. That left no choice but to join me in this egalitarian stance. I was hyper-organized with documents to highlight just enough details to explain the situation. I did not flood them with information.

Then I made my pitch. "Dana, I feel you are uniquely qualified to offer your insights about these two issues I can't seem to resolve. Both your history with the company and your expertise would be so helpful. I'd like to hear your thoughts."

Dana had gotten used to me in the past couple years and no longer saw me as such a newbie but they hadn't warmed up to me either. Presenting them with problems I needed to solve was a perfect win-

win. Dana was in their comfort zone and felt my respect and I was getting fantastic advice. We had an easy and lively discussion, moving into that place of rapport where there is a give and take, loads of questions, bouncing ideas off each other and even a bit of laughter. I could see how engaged Dana was the longer we talked.

When our time was up, I thanked them for everything and promised to circle back to let them know how things turned out. The icing came when Dana said, "This was fun. Don't wait so long to pull me in the next time. I'd love to jump in."

I never answered my original question about why Dana was so authoritarian and uptight. But I cracked through their armor and created a meaningful connection. As it happens, I turned to Dana repeatedly for their input. And they began to tap my brain too. All it took was patience, thoughtful observation, and the right approach, and I created a meaningful bond even with someone as icy as Dana.

A CHANCE TO
DO GOOD

One perk of being a big shot was that some interesting external opportunities appeared. I participated in public forums on a range of topics, joined a business round table group, and was asked to be a board member for other organizations. I wanted some board experience so I considered my options. I decided that my soul needed to help a worthy nonprofit. My yang was in bad need of some yin.

After much consideration, I joined a board that focused on early childhood education. I have a passion for giving kids an early leg up. I believe deep in my bones that reading opens all doors regardless of background, neighborhood or family the universe randomly plopped us into. This certainly was true for me. I struggled with reading until my first grade teacher spent extra time with me after school. She helped unlock the secret code of letters and words and exposed me to the magic of libraries. I felt this nonprofit board would give me the chance to pay the debt to my teacher and illuminate the path for other children.

I spent three years on the board and learned a tremendous amount. The biggest a-ha was how different the ethos is in a nonprofit. What I observed about the culture of the organization (and to a greater degree with the board) was the huge Urge for Pleasantries and Comfort. Disagreement, pushback, conflict, challenging the status quo? Not allowed. Change, experimentation, failure? Heaven forbid. The energy and intentions needed to remain a placid lake without any ripples. As you can imagine, this protocol was very hard for me. Actually, it was impossible. I did challenge board members. I did raise new ideas. I did question the value of certain programs. I did want to bring in new leaders to the organization. I made small dents but not the impact I was hoping for.

I formed a strong alliance with the Executive Director and was happy to be their sounding board. In time, I noticed that we always had the same conversation over and over again. Whether the topic was strategy or staffing or program excellence, the subtext was the same: "I want to do this great thing but it will upset the staff so I'm not going to move forward." When I pressed the ED to take the reins, to shake things up, not to cave to the real or imagined staff fragility, they only stepped up on occasion. I saw first-hand the outrageous over-reaction from the staff about the smallest amount of changes. They protested that the ED was wielding their power. (Duh?) They insisted that any decisions made by the leadership team were autocratic and did not account for the consensus of the staff. (So, they wanted a leaderless organization?) They policed the leaders' choice of words, ideas that were too innovative and even tough personnel decisions. (Inmates running the asylum?)

In my wildest dreams, I couldn't imagine any of these staff or leader behaviors flying at my day job. They were so far outside the norm of running any type of business. Despite themselves, this organization had modest success with some notoriety, which fucked with my head. If their culture and norms were so dysfunctional, how could they possibly succeed? My best guess is that nonprofits are a different beast and the outside world understands that and lets it be. I was trying to push the proverbial rock uphill but the rock was happy right where it was. This was not my cup of tea. I respectfully resigned when my term was up and traded my herbal tea for a good stiff drink.

But that wasn't the end of the story. The board chair spent six months trying to persuade me to stay. Phone calls, lunch meetings, pleading emails. Their point was how badly the organization needed my perspective, against-the-grain behavior, and skills. My response was those attributes were thoroughly rejected. The chair expressed their own frustration and wanted me to form an alliance to push forward. I was tempted to try harder because of my love for the mission.

But I just didn't see the value. I still walked away.

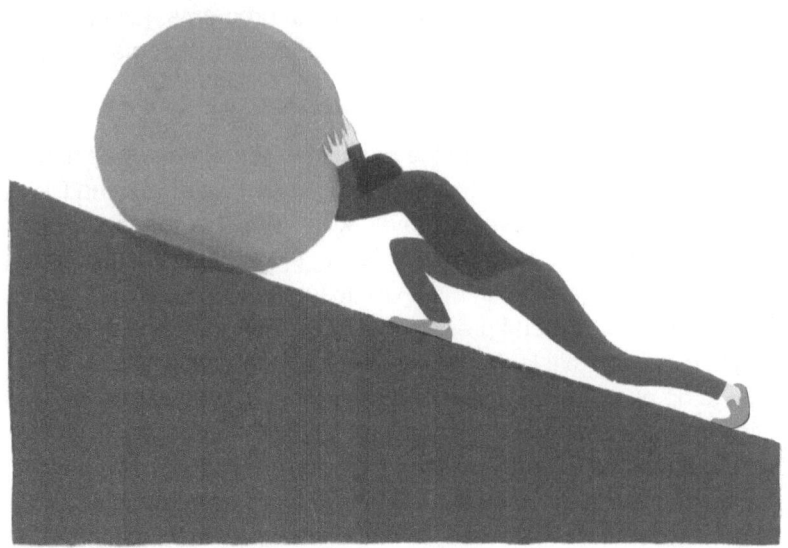

Since all of my experience had been in corporate-land, my foray into nonprofits was eye opening. The good news is it didn't dampen my love for these wonderful organizations. The bad news is I haven't served on another board. If corporations know too little about people stuff, nonprofits seem to have overcorrected. I'm still searching for a way to have an impact but I'm pretty sure that my square peg just doesn't fit their mold.

Big sigh.

DANGER AHEAD

With Terry gone and Robin still a question mark, the CEO did some reshuffling of the executive team, leaving an opening for some more fresh faces. One of my VP's, Lonnie, was perfect for the new role and I put their name forward. Resounding enthusiasm all around. That is, except from Bobbie. With venomous intent, they blocked the promotion single-handedly. When asked what their objections were to Lonnie, Bobbie simply stated they didn't like them. Others on the team pushed back while the CEO sat back and listened. Bobbie's veto power essentially put Lonnie out of the running. This was personal. Not about Lonnie, but about me. This was Bobbie's chance to hurt me.

The CEO reached out to me. "Micah, clearly there are no serious objections to Lonnie. This appears to be something between you and Bobbie. What can you tell me?"

Because we have a good relationship and because they had made some good changes, I felt I could be honest. "For some reason, Bobbie sees me as the competition. Since I joined this team, we haven't had many positive encounters or collaborations. They're openly hostile towards me and I have chosen not to bite. I just avoid Bobbie."

The CEO affirmed my perspective and I decided to stick my neck out. If my experience on my own team with Parker hadn't happened so recently, I might have let it pass, but now I felt compelled to speak up. Deep breath. "It's no secret in the organization that Bobbie doesn't think twice about causing harm to others. You've seen the talented people who have left us because of it. Bobbie's saving grace is how consistently they achieve impressive results. And it is that success that causes you and others to look away when Bobbie misbehaves. This is a long-term, chronic problem and I'm wondering when you are going to finally address the situation."

To my disappointment, the old, loyal, slow-moving version of the CEO resurfaced and responded to my candid feedback. "Of course, what you are saying is accurate. And I've known for a long time that I need to do something about it. But I feel ambivalent. I think the business will suffer if I remove Bobbie, yet I know they erode our culture. But I just can't seem to act. Plus, Bobbie and I have a history. We came up together and have a decent one-on-one relationship."

"I understand how you feel. This reminds me of my recent experience with Parker, who you helped me get rid of. The feedback my team gave me after the fact made me ashamed of my lack of courage. Everyone figured out how to ignore Parker, but they couldn't ignore *my* failings. They were appalled at my inaction. I have been regaining their trust slowly but surely. Bottom line. I wish I had made the move long ago."

Long pause. Finally, the CEO spoke up. "You've given me a great deal to think about. I guess I know what I'll be talking about with my coach this week."

The CEO asked their coach to speak with Bobbie. When the coach asked what were Bobbie's concerns about Lonnie, Bobbie was cagey. Then, when the coach asked if Bobbie's concerns had more to do with me, they sneered, "All the fancy interpersonal skills on the planet don't turn in great results." And so, the coach confirmed that Lonnie was collateral damage in Bobbie's attacks on me.

The CEO updated me during a conversation where they also asked me to "play nice" with Bobbie. The request made me snap. In a good way. I felt a calm come over me, suddenly clearly aware of what is right and wrong. I couldn't take shit anymore. My mind slowed down and I could see the words coming out of my mouth, my whole being unafraid and free of anxiety. It was pure zen.

"This is not my problem to solve. It's yours. I've been respectful and professional in my relationship with Bobbie. There's nothing more I can or will do." And then I got up and left the CEO's office. I had cleared enough of my own crap out of the way to objectively see the situation before me with little emotion. Let the chips fall where they may.

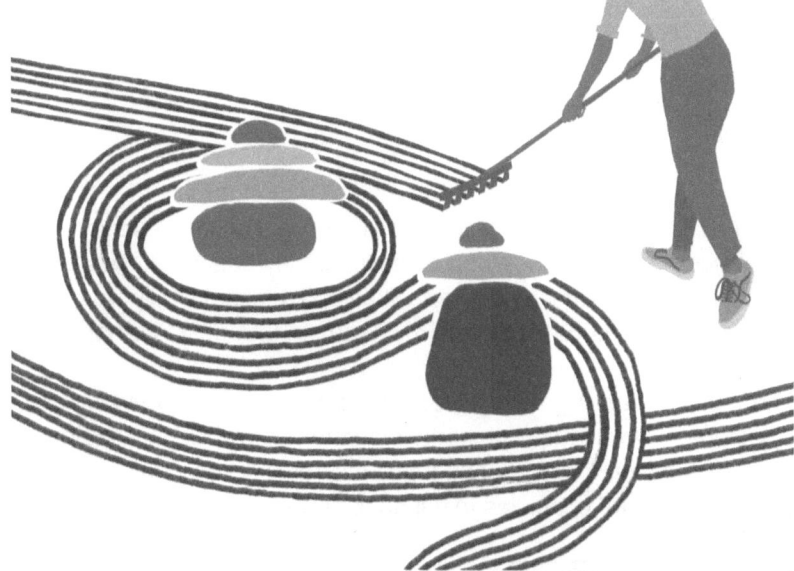

The CEO finally told Bobbie that they needed to clean up their act, or else. Bobbie was stunned and then pissed. Their behavior towards me got worse and they tried to gain allies from our team without success. As a result, Bobbie stormed into my office, angry that I had turned everyone against them. Bobbie threatened me as I escorted them out of my office. The CEO fired Bobbie the next day. Lonnie was promoted and new vitality infused our work. Even the CEO seemed lighter.

All the energy I used to protect myself was freed up to do bold and creative work. We can't bring our best selves to work when we need to prepare for battles lurking around every corner. Bobbie's exit con-firmed what I already knew: on a team without shitheads, great stuff can happen.

AND ALL THAT JAZZ

With Parker gone, my team was humming. Sometimes they hummed Beethoven and sometimes they busted out some Bob Marley. But mostly it was Coltrane-like improv jazz. I finally was part of a team experience that made my heart sing. Usually Aretha.

I remember watching Saku's team years ago and being envious of what looked like magic. I came to understand that "magic" requires deliberate action, practice, and many failures. By this point, I was certain of several principles that lead to successful teams.

A team needs a purpose and some goals. Otherwise, why waste the time being together? I figured out that the more passion the team has for the purpose, the more drive they will have to reach the goals. I didn't get this earlier in my career. I was too wishy-washy and couldn't understand why people bitched all the time about having to show up. Now I realize what their complaints really meant, in the immortal words of Luther Vandross, "Give Me a Reason".

I read all the research and inspirational books about creating a cohesive team no matter who the members were. I thought it was possible to take 3rd string players and elevate their game with just the right coaching. Chris showed me that was bullshit and that the best teams only develop when the best people are on them. Period. The bottom line: teams will gravitate towards the lowest common denominator more frequently than they will lift up the weakest members.

Seriously, what leader looks at the roster of possible team members and says, "I think I'll take that loser over there instead of that star"?

My hardest lessons had to do with managing (or removing) all the personalities. I had an inflated sense of my abilities to reform bad behavior, and deep denial that shitty people could create lasting damage. I did great at bringing out the best in folks as long as they weren't psychopaths. When members act like normal people, it is much easier to address the ordinary ups and downs that are part of team life.

With a compelling purpose, the best people, and reasonable person-alities, it's possible to facilitate exciting conversations and collective problem solving. It took me awhile, but I had finally absorbed what I had observed and learned from Saku. My team had that special something and it had very little to do with me. My ego was happy not-happy about this. Happy because it was satisfying and humbling to watch my team. Not happy because I couldn't claim any glory.

Note to Self: If I was doing a fantastic job as a leader and achieving great results, it was because my people were on fire. I was more invisible with the occasional whisper. It was no longer about me in the spotlight.

A NIFTY TRICK

Speaking of teams, Yael hatched an initiative that the senior team rallied around. We developed an innovation contest for the whole organization. We invited everyone to form cross-functional groups to generate pitches for new products or processes. We set parameters and guidelines, and each group had an executive advisor. At the end of three months, each group presented their ideas to the entire staff. After everyone made their pitch, all staff voted to select winners, who received monetary rewards and the resources to implement their plans.

It wasn't the outline of the program or the motivational rewards that led to its success. It wasn't the senior involvement although that was a huge help. It wasn't the time or resources that were granted although that helped too. It was how Yael framed the challenge and inspired the troops. Something I wish I could do as effectively.

Yael painted a picture that ignited the imagination of the audience without hyperbole or tap dancing or flash. They aimed straight for the guts and made everyone in the organization believe they were capable of bold, creative, novel thinking that would revolutionize some aspect of the business.

Yael's message was simple. There are big problems to solve, new uncharted terrain to explore, advances to make and cool things yet to invent. There is no "they" who will do this work. There is only "us", all of us. Some ideas will pop up and fizzle, others will take hold. Some will be born from frustration with the status quo, others from the ether. Joining forces to test, discuss and debate options will reveal the best of the best. Whatever the results, the process will be persuasive. It will convince each person of their capacity to think and act in new ways. And won't we all be better off when that happens?

Yael taught the executive team the Do-Nothing strategy. As they put it, "Sometimes doing nothing brings about the best outcomes. If you just sit back and trust that your people can sort things out for themselves, you'd be surprised how often the right thing happens." I often remind myself of this golden nugget of wisdom. Someone rushes into my office begging for explicit guidance. All that comes out of my mouth is, "That's interesting. I bet you can figure this out" and then I send them on their way. Or I get frantic emails that I just don't return. What I learned from Yael is, "if you don't intervene, your people will be forced to step up." I wish I had known this a long time ago. All those years of Leadership Enabling Dependency! Where is the 12-step program for that?

Life was good. My team was the envy of all, the executive team had improved and I was hitting my stride. I felt that I was integrating all the ups and downs, good and bad role models and a-ha moments in my growth as a leader. I felt less worried that I was going to fuck up or be blindsided. Although I had put away my superhero cape, I felt confident that I could handle anything that came along.

OPPORTUNITY KNOCKS

Although I received many calls from headhunters, I politely declined. I was in a comfortable groove and wanted to take a breath at the company, but I was getting a little bored. So, when a call came through about being the CEO of a mid-sized technology company, my ears perked up. At first I had reservations: Tech? Me? Pat had taught me a lot over the years but only enough to not sound like an idiot.

They hooked me by speaking *my* language, "We are looking for someone who has great people skills. We've heard you speak at conferences and read some great articles about you."

Was that my chest puffing up? Was that my ego dying to come out and play? Was that my superhero cape peeking out of my drawer? Of course, I was flattered. But I was older and wiser and wasn't about to fall for my own bullshit. Before I went for the first interview, I made sure that my vanity was under lock and key and kept an eye out for any red flashing warning signs.

This company was on the verge of shutting the gap but was held back by an inability to have new ideas and productive debates. They had the talent and an impressive track record but the business was about to stall out. The board assessed that a very different type of leader needed to take the reins. Voila. C'est moi.

Thankfully, I was close friends with my flaws at this stage of my career. I could see them coming a mile away. As the board and headhunter began their hard sell, I made my terms clear to them. 1) I wanted to bring Rene in as my number two person. 2) I wanted to spend the first six months assessing the talent, culture and obstacles so I could move on critical changes within the first year. 3) I wanted Sydney's help for the first year. 4) I wanted regular time with the board chair. They agreed to my terms and I began my transition.

My last month on the executive team was bittersweet. Jules, Cam, Yael and Pat were very excited for me but sad to see me go. The feeling was mutual. Jules and I had a fantastic dinner at a new restaurant to celebrate. Cam finally revealed that Pat was the buddy that reached out to them. Yael told me that they were being recruited too but wasn't sure what to do. And Pat chuckled softly when they heard I was going to be heading a tech company. I proclaimed it was all their fault. Dana and I had formed an unexpected bond that had changed both of us. Robin was still distant and Lonnie was grateful I had opened doors for them. With each colleague, I shared how much I had learned from them and how they made me a better leader. I was pleased to learn that I had an impact on them as well.

In my heartfelt last conversation with the CEO, I thanked them for all the opportunities, for listening to me, and for letting me just be Micah. I was not expecting what they shared with me.

"When I first met you I was struck by your ability to maintain your unique sense of self despite the pressure to blend in. I watched you closely to learn how this is done. You know yourself, you aren't afraid to voice your thoughts, even if they are out of the mainstream. And you are able to get others to pay attention to the right things. You cut through the noise. This is because you listen to others and treat them with respect. Once that mutual rapport is in place, it grants you license to push people to consider new perspectives and try new actions. You take closed minds and systems and open them up. You certainly had that effect on me. I saw in you the leader the company needed and I had to work to catch up. I can't thank you enough."

Even after all those years struggling to stay true to my square pegged-ness, I still felt shocked by the CEO's observations. I succeeded in staying true to myself. I decided to spend time with Sydney to reflect on my growth up to this point and what I needed to do to set myself up for success as a CEO.

"Sydney, I think I need to hit the pause button and think about what I've learned about myself as a leader up to this point and what I need to do going forward. The stakes are higher now. The buck stops with me and many livelihoods depend on me. I feel up to the task but I've come to know my shortcomings and I want to avoid big slip-ups."

"You're right. The role of the CEO is unique. All eyes will be on you in ways you haven't experienced before. When you blink, people will give that catastrophic meaning. When you think out loud, people will hear that as Moses handing down the tablets. When you show up late for a meeting, it will be clear that nothing can happen without you. The tiniest things will be magnified and misinterpreted. Being under the microscope isn't one of your strengths. In fact, it annoys you.

"Let's take stock first. Let's do a lightning round: I'll ask you a question and you respond with the first thing that comes to mind. Don't censor yourself. First question: What is your greatest strength as a leader?"

"Bringing other people along for the ride. Valuing, listening, enlisting others."

"Do you ever do too much of that?"

"Sometimes. Not everything needs to be a conversation. My dilemma stems from a worry that I will exert too much power or control. I've certainly been burned by dictator-types in the past and I failed miserably when I tried to employ that approach myself. I know, I overcorrected. Next question."

"What's your biggest blind spot? What keeps taking you by surprise?"

"Not everyone has good intentions. I'm still amazed when people do shitty things to other people. I'm not quite as trusting as I used to be but I still don't see it coming. I suppose it wouldn't be the worst epitaph to have etched on my gravestone: Here lies Micah who believed that people are basically good."

Sydney chuckled and asked the next question. "What is still your biggest challenge as a leader?"

"Politics," I blurted. "I learned a lot more as an SVP, especially watching people like Cam and Jules. Cam made it look effortless and Jules knew which battles to pick. In politics, there are winners and losers. I still struggle to find the win-win when the dynamics shift away from problem solving and veer into face-saving."

"From your experience, what are the two or three most important things you learned a leader must do?"

"What my first mentor, Shante, impressed upon me; to know myself with brutal honesty, find meaning and purpose in the work and gain the respect and involvement of others. They also told me to act with humility and compassion. I had no fucking clue what Shante was talking about. I would say I've been working on developing these traits all these years."

"What would you say was your biggest misconception about leading?"

"Everything! I left grad school thinking that developing a great strategy, implementing project plans, innovating and using big data effectively was the definition of great leadership. I came to learn that those were tools that didn't have shit to do with leading. Sure, leaders need to use those tools to achieve results but without other skills learned from experience, the results won't meet high expectations, let alone exceed them. I must have missed the class where they told us that leaders lead a "Who", not a "What". I thought if I was proficient at all the "Things", the "Human Stuff" would take care of itself. I can't point to a single leader I encountered who excelled at all the "What's" and none of the "Who's" but was still a great leader."

Sydney was ready to move on. "Okay, now let's think ahead to taking the Big Seat. When you were a VP, what is the one thing you wanted more than anything from the CEO?"

Hmmm. "I wanted them to *Be the Change* and not just *Direct the Change*. I recognized the CEO's good intentions and inspiring words. But when it came to the hard stuff, like dealing with the assholes who were undermining the transformation efforts or changing the CEO's own behavior, they disappointed me. I struggled to respect them because they lacked the courage and fortitude that they expected from the rest of us. I wanted them to have the balls to do the right thing."

"What will you do to ensure that you embody the efforts you are asking others to take on?"

"I can't ask others to do anything that I don't do first. You know how parents yell at their kids to put down their phones while they're on their own phones? Do kids pay attention to the words or the actions? So, going forward, first I change my behavior and then I open my mouth."

"You are walking into a situation where you will be viewed as the odd duck because you did not come up in the tech world. How will you gain the staff's respect?"

"Being the odd duck is in my comfort zone so that won't be new. But I will be on a steep learning curve to assimilate into this new sector. I need to find that balance between pummeling my staff with questions and not looking like a complete neophyte. They will get exhausted and it will make me look incompetent. They will lose confidence in me out of the gate. So, I think initially I will listen to what everyone has to say, and then share my own expertise. I need to show everyone why the board selected me over one of their own."

"That's a good start, Micah, but let's dig deeper into this. You need to make sure you capture their imagination and receptivity immediately. Tell me your thoughts about the first several weeks versus several months."

"I only have one chance to make a good first impression. Right. Hmmm. I guess the forum would be an all-staff meeting? And I need to speak their language, not mine. I need to meet them where they are rather than the reverse. Help me out here. What else?"

"Are you saying that being yourself, the thing that got you to where you are now, isn't going to work in this situation? I believe there is evidence that being Micah is a good strategy for you. When you have stepped outside of yourself things have not gone well. So, tell me what a "Micah" launch into the CEO role looks like."

Snarky, self-effacing, direct, no bullshit. But I couldn't let them see that on day one. Or could I? Did I think I needed to dial it back because of my new role as the CEO? Did I think I needed to become more of a gearhead and less of a human being? I knew I would never be as tech savvy as the staff so why would I even try? And they had asked me to join their team because I was not like them. My task was to help them develop some new skills and ways of working together that I was uniquely qualified to lead. Wow, without realizing it, I was going down the rabbit hole, and if I wasn't careful, I might never escape my own self-doubt.

"For some reason, I'm worried that being Totally Micah is unbecoming to the role of CEO. How did this happen?"

"I think there are misconceptions about the role that cause most CEOs to take on a scripted persona. You know the one. Set the vision, inspire the troops, determine the objectives, don't reach out too much, delegate, stay opaque. All the things that fulfill the "lonely at the top" prophecy. But I think you know from your own experience what staff truly needs and it isn't a prefab leader. They want connection and engagement from the CEO."

"So, if I use my strengths to tune into staff needs, then I'm on firm ground. Don't focus so much on the stuff I don't know yet."

"And remember the conversation we had a while back about executive team dynamics. Leaders will be jockeying for favored status with you and trying to hold onto their power. Your team may be a bit squirrely until everyone settles into the new normal under your leadership."

"I'm so glad we had this conversation. I need some time to digest this and be sure that I launch into this new role being the leader I want to be."

It amazed me how, no matter how much I grew and changed, I would always have more to learn and adapt. Good news-bad news. It's great because we need to keep evolving. Otherwise, we'd be fully baked by age 30. Imagine being stalled at that point in development! A needy puppy dog in search of constant affirmation who thinks they are The It. At the same time, constant growth can be tough. All that self-reflection, taking feedback seriously, owning up to flaws, trying new perspectives and actions. How fucking exhausting. At the end of the day, though, I'd be lying if I said it wasn't worth it.

SUPER MICAH
TO THE RESCUE

By the time I started my new job, I had a launch plan that felt true to myself. A mixture of making connections, offering straight talk, pulling together the team, letting the staff get a taste of the real me, and loads of listening.

I started with my executive team. My goal was to develop a relationship with each person and to learn as much as possible about their roles and their hopes and concerns for the company. I scheduled informal lunches outside the building for each conversation to keep it chill.

All eight people were wicked smart and had clear thoughts about where the company needed to go next. Of course, there were six different versions of that future and twenty opinions about what held us back. They were open and eager to give their input.

Then it came time for me to share my thoughts. I could read the skepticism on their faces and they didn't even bother to push back or ask questions. Shit. Sydney was right. Winning over a group of people who saw me as a stupid outsider was going to be harder than I imagined. The younger version of myself would have been downright indignant. How could they not see how fantastic I was for this company? But the mature Micah understood the situation and even had a few ideas about how to blast through this.

Once I completed all my individual conversations, I gathered the team together for our first meeting. I assumed they had all spoken privately with each other and shared a consensus that the board made a horrible mistake. I needed to make them question that conclusion.

When they walked into the meeting room, they were surprised to see that I had replaced the long rectangular table with a round one. I made sure that I was the last one to sit down. I had no idea what the pecking order was but I'm certain I disrupted it. I also shut down all electronic devices. I didn't say one word about the change of scenery. I just proceeded.

"First of all, I want to thank everyone for your time and candor during our discussions in the past couple weeks. They were very illuminating. And secondly, I want to say how excited I am to join you. This is an outstanding company; you've done remarkable things and the future is full of opportunity.

"I didn't have a chance to share much about myself in our meetings so I'd like to introduce myself to you by sharing a couple stories that will tell you more than my resume. About nine years ago I was in charge of a major software upgrade for the company. I was like one of your customers. It was a very visible, expensive and do-or-die initiative. I did all the right things—or so I thought. Partnering with the vendor, internal planning and commitments, engaging key players, lots of analysis and customization. Five months of deep planning and it looked like everything was good to go. It was a disaster and the blame fell on me. Despite this screw up, I managed to salvage the project and my reputation, but it wasn't easy. I conducted a post-mortem with the team. Can anyone guess what the number one error was?"

I waited patiently. Finally, someone offered, "You made a bad vendor selection?" Someone else chimed in, "You didn't know enough about the system to ask the right questions?" Three more ideas about what I had done wrong.

I responded, "Actually, the team determined that any miscalculations we made were an outcome of the vendor over-selling and under-listening. The main error was that the vendor promised to attend to our specific needs and they failed miserably. I learned a great deal from that experience but these are the two biggies. For one, there is no finger-pointing in leadership. Just taking responsibility. And secondly, tech companies are not good at partnering with their clients."

I let that sink in for a moment and then continued. "More recently I had the pleasure of working closely with a tech genius. Pat was one of my peers on the executive team at my last company. From the moment we got to know each other, we were struck by how our differences created unusual approaches and solutions to the work. We struggled initially to find a common language, but in the end we settled on plain English. Some of the most interesting and innovative work of my career happened in collaboration with Pat. When I was saying my goodbyes, we agreed that we had both been coming from a one-dimensional space. Our thinking had become insular and our contributions were predictable. We made each other better and we breathed new life into our abilities to lead and take on big issues. I would say that my learning and association with Pat is the main reason I am sitting at this table with you. Tech companies need more people like me and people like me need more exposure to companies like you. It is a dynamic combination that few organizations have figured out. Tech companies that excel at this secret formula are the ones that will crush it in the marketplace.

"And that's why I'm so excited about what we can do together. We can be one of the first and surprise the crap out of our competition."

The non-verbals changed considerably. Dare I say, there was even a spark of excitement and curiosity. But I wasn't done setting the (round) table.

"So, that's me in a nutshell. Now I want to tell you what I heard from all of you. Let me state the obvious. You are all crazy smart and accomplished. I lost count of the number of patents held by people at this table. And you all share enthusiasm and optimism about the future of the company. Your can-do attitude is infectious. The unanimity falls apart in diagnosing what obstacles are present and what to do about them.

"There was a common theme, however. Everyone expressed a sense that responsibility for difficulties fell on someone other than themselves, and that once others took action, things would improve. I didn't hear one person take a holistic view of the organization or fess up to some personal or departmental shortcoming. Lots of finger-pointing. And I've already told you what I think about that. Leadership is never about blaming others. We own our teams' problems. We put our heads together to solve issues. We are in this together. If we aren't, we will never realize our fullest potential."

Wait for it. Wait for it. "It sounds like we all need to brush up on our plain English," offered the person to my right. Laughter all around; not all of it the happy kind. But the ice was broken and I had put them off balance. I needed to create reasonable doubt or the element of surprise or a magic trick. While they were still tipsy, I jumped back in.

"With that as the backdrop, I'd like to imagine my introduction to the company as a reset of sorts. I'd like to start immediately developing that secret formula to marry all our tech expertise with more relationship building skills to enhance our brand. I want our team to create a new message that we can use when I formally kick off my tenure at our all-staff meeting. It will become our shared mantra and behavior going forward."

And with that, I skipped right over any objections that I knew hung in the air and facilitated an interesting discussion. It wasn't the best but it was a start. I remembered my conversation with Sydney and the need to make a unique first impression. It was clear that they were not used to the round table, the open sharing from the CEO, the pressure to work as a collective unit and the no-bullshit attitude. My biggest coup was not giving unlimited oxygen to the Airing of Grievances. So, not only was I presenting this team with a new experience but I was also trying to live out my own aspirations. I wanted to finally do what I wished for all along.

Deep cleansing breath.

ANOTHER ASSHOLE

My first six months were total immersion. My life outside of work disappeared as I drank from the fire hydrant, absorbed as much as possible and got my footing. The staff quickly understood that I was different and they weren't sure what to make of me. My team was adapting to my style of leadership but we weren't knit together yet. I spent loads of one-on-one time developing my relationships with each of them. I exhibited more patience than usual for this task. So, it's not true what they say about old dogs.

Now it was time to engage my team to commit to a new direction. Having Rene as my right hand made a tough task smooth as but-tah. As I've mentioned before, it is impossible to say no to Rene. They have a way of making things sound exciting, possible, and compelling. I had Rene warm people up privately before the team meeting.

I wanted the team to walk out of a two-day offsite feeling a tighter bond with each other and enthusiasm for where we were headed. High hopes, I know, but what's wrong with dreaming big? I wanted to jumpstart a new way of doing business. I wanted to shock the system a bit. So, I spent time reflecting on what I knew worked and didn't work. I had only one agenda item: develop closer bonds between the team members. Share stories, learn things they didn't know, start to care about each other.

We didn't do ropes or trust falls or cooking class. We just spent two days telling story after story. Everyone laughed, cried, suffered a bit of heartbreak, and gushed compassion. We started slowly, and by day two, I could tell that the entire group felt a strong desire to learn more about each other. It went better than I could have imagined. I wanted to prove that when people feel connected and care about each other, it becomes more difficult to screw each other over and that it is more likely they will collaborate as a team.

And that is what happened. The turf battles decreased, checking in with each other increased, the meetings were more stimulating, tensions and misunderstandings eased. Conversations flowed more easily. New ideas emerged and people felt comfortable debating them openly and honestly. The team was turning a corner.

Several months into our New Beginning, I sensed something was off. I noticed some eye rolling, a bit of sniping and some withdrawal from a couple members. I needed to nip this in the bud so I asked Rene to do some reconnoitering. My spidey-senses were right; something was going on and it wasn't pretty.

"Micah, you're not going to like this. It seems that Dylan (EVP, New Products) has been bad-mouthing you all over the place. They were skeptical when you arrived but ever since the offsite, they have gone from skeptical to mocking. The basic message is 'the new CEO is a nutcase who doesn't have a clue about tech and spends too much time on people bullshit.' Dylan is shouting at anyone who will listen."

"Do you have a sense if they are gaining recruits? Or is there push-back?"

"It's hard to say. Dylan certainly has supporters and respect, but so do you. When I spoke with the other EVPs, they downplayed it. I guess Dylan is seen as a naysayer and back-stabber. The team hopes you will deal with Dylan."

Shit! I was hoping I wouldn't have to deal with this so early in the job. I thanked Rene for the update and put in a call to Sydney.

Sydney asked, "What are you going to do about it?"

"Obviously, a private conversation with Dylan to start. I'll let them know that information filtered back to me and ask them to explain. Make them do most of the talking. Make it clear that this is unaccept-able and I won't let it stand if it keeps happening."

"Yep. What happens if they apologize and swear it will never happen again?"

"Create a plan for observation and verification that Dylan has kept their word. And let them know the consequences of not shaping up."

"Ah, you are older and wiser. I assume you know what you will do if they persist in undermining you."

"I've got to do what my previous boss did. I know it is the right thing to do but I worry about the fallout. I'm still new, still trying to establish credibility, and I'm not sure how it will be received." Sydney and I talked it through some more and then I set up a meeting with Dylan.

Turns out Dylan was a serious saboteur and they weren't afraid to get up in my face. I had HR draw up severance papers, and Dylan left the company within the week. I convened the senior team for a brief meeting.

I wanted to share the story on my own terms. "As you know, I had to let Dylan go. I became aware of their lack of support for me and the direction our team is taking. They confirmed that what I heard was true and went on to provide an extensive critique. It became clear that nothing was going to change their mind so we agreed to sever them from the company. I am disappointed this occurred but I won't allow anyone or anything to jeopardize our collective success. I won't allow corrosive behavior. It hurts our team."

I let that hang out there to see if anyone would speak up. It only took a moment before the dam burst. I received a verbal standing ovation. Dylan had been a pain in everyone's ass for a long time and they wondered how long it would take before I discovered that. They had all been on the receiving end of Dylan's crappy behavior but the previous CEO didn't manage it.

While I was enjoying the glow as their Conquering Hero, I asked for the team's help. "As clear as I am about letting Dylan go, I'm worried about two things. Who takes charge of new products and how will the staff react? I don't want any disruption to the business and I need us to close ranks to make sure that doesn't happen."

They offered three great suggestions about who could fill the role, an interim solution for a key project and ideas about how to describe this event to the staff. They persuaded me that most of the organization would be relieved that Dylan was gone and that my stock would go up. Phew! I told the team I wanted to move through this transition as a united team. They were on board. Thank you lord for a wildly successful bonding offsite. The dividends were already paying off.

ATOP OLYMPUS:
THE BOARD

Before I left my old job, I asked the CEO to give me a tutorial on dealing with the Board of Directors. I had very little exposure or knowledge and I needed to get smart quickly. They were very generous with their guidance. It boiled down to three things: developing alliances with the chair and other members, being proficient discussing the numbers and telling the truth early if there was bad news ahead. Despite my confidence in these abilities, interacting with a board is a different beast. Accountability and performance are constantly measured. I worried that I would freak out under the constant glare. So, I did what I do best: started developing a personal connection with each board member.

I set up monthly dinners with the chair, hoping to develop a bond to help both of us feel comfortable. I'm not going to lie; I was nervous as shit. It's one thing to arrive at the Grown Ups' Table and another to become the CEO and know that my actions could make or break our success. This required a Superpower I hadn't developed.

Blair, the chairperson, knew my story before they urged the whole board to hire me. They knew about my lack of experience working with a board, and Blair was ready to be helpful. Phew. Our dinner conversations were broad *and* deep. I learned more about the history of the company; huge wins and colossal failures. I got a sense of the current executives and board members and what Blair thought of them. We talked about growth strategies, business risks, market share, brand issues, compensation and culture. It was clear that the board had been good guardians.

One regret that Blair shared was letting the previous CEO stay on despite many warning signs. (I guess sorting out what to do with brilliant assholes goes all the way up the chain! Who knew?) They said this person's reputation in the sector was formidable so the board had to grapple with which damage the company could withstand; the internal mass exodus of top talent or external gossip and brand erosion. There were long and difficult conversations before the board placed its bet. Blair and others were still circling the industry wagons and hoping that this would be a minor blip.

This brand management effort turned into our first joint venture. Blair and I agreed to present together at several industry meetings. We spent hours crafting our message and landed on a way to signal that the whole sector, not just our company, needed to wake up. We controlled the narrative that we *needed* to change leaders in order to chart a new course. We didn't bad-mouth or finger-point; we simply challenged the industry to progress into the future.

We rocked it! This roadshow served several purposes. I was introduced to my peers in the sector by a very supportive board chair, Blair and I bonded in ways that would be very useful during the inevitable tough times ahead, the board felt relieved about our damage control efforts and the staff saw that I had some serious chops.

Even though I enjoyed good relationships with the board, I found our quarterly board meetings nerve wracking. I relied heavily on the CFO, legal and HR to prepare for these events and delivered all the relevant information that was required. I was a dutiful CEO for the first three quarters but I just didn't know if I could survive this drill every few months. Reviewing reams of documents they could read on their own was a waste of time and talent. I had to shake things up. I know, you're shocked.

At one of our dinners, I broached the topic with Blair. I wondered if they ever wished we had deeper discussions about Big Stuff like the future or trends nipping at our heels or ways to have a positive impact on humanity. They bitched about the retrospective nature of board meetings and their intense desire to tap this group's collective genius about what's around the next corner. So, we hatched another plan.

Board members received their quarterly documents two weeks before the meeting with instructions to review them and submit any questions or concerns one week before the meeting. Blair and I culled through the list and invited relevant staff members to address the issues on the first day. By late afternoon, a consultant took over the proceedings. Over a casual dinner, everyone was asked to riff on a Big Stuff question. It was loose and informal and meant as a warm up to the next day. Day two was a highly structured, expansive discussion that tapped the knowledge and insights of the whole board. At the end of the day, the consultant asked one question. What is the one thing the company is not yet doing that must begin immediately? There wasn't a complete consensus around one item but there was a cluster of themes that went together. We agreed that I would take this back to the executive team and give an informal status update before our next board meeting.

This board directive launched my team into new territory. It was a mix of excitement, frustration, tension and creativity. It took time before a serious plan emerged. When we were ready, the entire executive team met with the board for a couple days of examination and refinement. The team then made changes, allocated resources, and the board blessed the plan. This was an ambitious undertaking for the leadership team and the staff. There was risk as well as great potential. The journey was not a straight line. We had to course correct and recalculate expectations. In the end, it was a game changer for the company and we made a bit of a splash in the industry.

Without Blair and greater input from the board, this never would have occurred. I never imagined that a board was more than an obligation or a noose. I was so wrong! I hadn't heard of other companies where the boards were so engaged and generous with ideas and guidance. I think I lucked out with Blair. They sought me out to become the CEO, they were invested in my success and they were willing to switch things up. Maybe the moral of the story is that CEO's and board chairs need to establish a close working relationship and then prod each other to experiment. Or maybe this is just about my own impatience and inability to sit through two day meetings going over numbers!

Just so you know, things with the board aren't always this wonderful. We've had shitty quarters, I get beat up routinely and I'm forced to squeeze out better margins. We do have meetings only about results and overhead expenses. But, on balance, I'm a fortunate son of a bitch.

MICAH LEARNS THE SUPERPOWER OF VULNERABILITY

One year into my tenure as CEO, I had some wins and disappointments on the scoreboard. In the win column, the senior team was developing into a powerhouse. They got me and were having fun working more collaboratively. I was able to sit back and listen to them wrestle with tough issues and come to good resolutions. We didn't always succeed but we were learning as we went along. The business gained several new and important customers and the staff was doing a bang-up job responding more accurately to their needs. We were knee-deep into our board-sponsored initiative. On the down side, we lost two customers to our competition and one of our product pilots was a bust. On balance, we were ahead of where things were when I arrived. Not too shabby for my first year.

Mid-way through year two, I suffered a personal loss. My best friend died from cancer and it hit me very hard. I talked with Sydney about how to deal with this at work. I agreed that pretending that I was "just fine" was going to be impossible, so I decided to be vulnerable.

At the start of our next senior team meeting, I told everyone I needed to share something. "You may have noticed that I'm off my game in the past several weeks. I've been struggling with the death of my life-long best friend. One day they called to say they had stage four cancer and two months later they died. I made several trips during those months to visit them and two weeks ago I went to the funeral.

Honestly, I'm a mess. I feel like one of my appendages is missing. I'm having a hard time focusing at work. I just wanted to let you know what is going on and to ask for some patience if I miss a few beats." The lump in my throat made it hard to say more and I started to tear up.

Through my watery gaze, I saw sympathetic faces. At first, no one spoke. Even in private, people struggle with talking about death; in this professional setting, my staff sat with the sad and surprising news. Slowly, people offered their support and stories about their own best friends.

For weeks afterwards, team members offered small acts of kindness. A latte, two sentenced supportive emails, lots of "need any help today?" and running our meetings. As I worked through my grief, I touched base again with Sydney.

I felt particularly reflective. "It's so interesting to me that showing up as a real human being, expressing vulnerability about real life stuff, and taking the risk to be emotional creates such a different dynamic. I've always been disciplined about putting on my game face at work and leaving my personal stuff at home. And before you say anything, I know that is hypocritical! I know that I encourage others to be real and that I am especially responsive to their concerns. It's not that I've never been revealing but it strikes me now that I usually share something from the past. I talk about something that I no longer feel vulnerable about; it's been worked through. But this grief is so pressing that I can't tuck it away. Although I feel uncomfortable walking around in this fog, I see some advantages to it."

Sydney nodded and let me continue. "By revealing my pain, I became relatable to my team. Being more approachable has allowed them to raise knottier issues with me and express some of their own emotions. It has strengthened their relationships with me. I've been so focused on making sure they bond with each other that I wasn't risking enough in my connections with each of them. I haven't been in this place before at work, except with my closest peers. I don't know that this is sustainable, but I can imagine dropping my guard again when life happens."

"Vulnerability is the key to good relationships," Sydney replied. "We can't establish meaningful connections without it. We have this notion that leaders can't show any cracks in their veneer. That it would be a sign of weakness. It's actually just the opposite. Strength requires a willingness to be vulnerable. It takes courage to risk exposing ourselves. Being tough is easy and, ultimately, a less effective leadership strategy. Micah, I'm impressed that you didn't pretend you were just fine with your team."

"If we weren't in such a good place, I probably would have tried harder to suck it up. Truth be told, not having to fake it has helped me get through each day. I just don't have the extra energy to put on a happy face."

Looking back, this moment was a turning point for me and the team. I was more relaxed, less worried about proving myself, more willing to say "I don't know" and (oddly) more confident. The more I was Total Micah, the more effective I became. And the more my team experienced Total Micah, the more they opened up too.

STATUS UPDATE
AND A BIT OF
WISDOM

I'm still CEO, the company is doing well and that's about all that has remained stable. Rene is now the CEO at another company. We get together monthly to exchange stories and provide support and laughter. My team has said goodbye to a few and hello to others. The board and I headed off a hostile takeover and we are now debating how much to grow the business. The culture is more collaborative and creative and staff are more satisfied.

I'm still learning how to be an effective leader. Most days I like the opportunity to grow and some days it exhausts me. I figure I'll move on or retire when I get bored with the whole thing. For now, I'm content.

I know you are expecting to find a pithy, succinct and clever summary here that tells you the secrets to leadership. I know you are dying for the quintessential list of "just do these five easy things" to become a fucking god among leaders. Sorry to disappoint you. Not gonna happen. As Shante told me all those years ago, leadership is about acute self-awareness and creating meaningful connections to people. And that ain't easy. In fact, it's quite messy. So, this is the Micah list which is decidedly not simple, for the faint-hearted or the uncommitted.

Leading is a deeply personal journey. If it's not, then you're probably not very effective. Most days I came home and obsessed about what I said to people. Was my tone too sharp? Was I clear enough? Was I too serious or not serious enough? Was I certain the team was with me? What do I need to circle back about and do differently tomorrow? Granted, we all know I can be a bit dramatic, but daily moments of self-reflection helped me course-correct. Being sure my ego was in check, that I listened more than talked or that I asked for help allowed me to evolve and get better over the years. I did not know this walking in. I did not do a good job of it early on. I just didn't know very much about myself. The help I got came in many forms; generous colleagues, willing mentors, an invaluable coach, good bosses, bad bosses, my own failures, my successes.

If you're in it for personal glory, that will suck for the people around you. You know the adage "you can only lead if you have followers". It turns out that people don't want to follow assholes, egomaniacs, manipulators, limelight hogs, or bullshitters. I took turns at being some of these and was on the receiving end of others. As I grew as a leader, I allowed myself to step back while my team was out front. Absolutely nothing gets done by a single person. You know, like my earlier version of myself as a superhero. You'll be pleased to know that my cape went into the recycle bin. I just wish I had done it sooner.

Show up as a multi-dimensional, complicated, flawed, vulnerable human being. I had a serious a-ha moment when I worked for Quinn. As always, I was working hard to pull my team together. But something just wasn't clicking into place. I tried every trick in the books in an attempt to connect better to my folks. I was using Rene as my sounding board, venting about how stand- offish everyone was. In their usual unnerving style, Rene asked, "Do you ever let them see you sweat? Do they have any sense of your concerns? Do you ever come out from behind your mask?" I responded defensively. "I need to gain their respect. I have to be what Quinn expects me to be. They'll think I'm weak if I waver." Rene wasn't having any of it. "Stop, Micah. How can you expect anyone to connect with you if you aren't tossing out any hooks for them to latch onto? All you've offered is Micah The Boss. Flat, unapproachable, not very likeable. Would you want to work hard for you?" And this is why I adore Rene. Tough love, wise advisor, cuts through my shit. From that day forward, I stopped working so hard to be a role instead of a real person.

I wasn't always sure that being Total Micah was the right formula. Too unconventional, too challenging, too square pegged. In short, too human. It took a long time and lots of practice to realize that being fully human was one of my greatest assets. I had to unlearn the idea that leaders needed to be...Just These Five Things. Those five things are valuable, no doubt, but they are tools or techniques.

There isn't a to-do list that helps you reveal your human beingness. And it is that humility, compassion, imperfection and fullness of being that helped me become an effective leader. When you think about it, don't you want everyone to show up for work filled with optimism, concern for others and the knowledge that we are all just human beings? Without that, we'd all be robots.

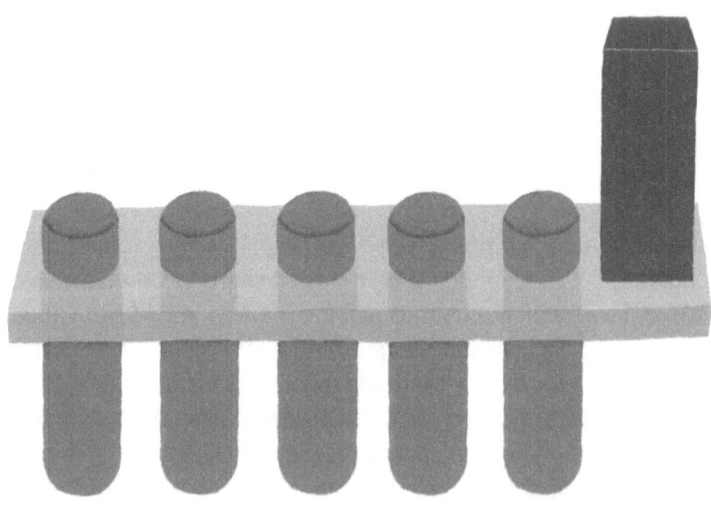

Bottom line: I needed to change myself before asking others to change. Which reminds me of a Hindu story I heard many years ago.

A frantic mother brought her young son to a very wise swami. "Baba-ji, please help me. From the time he wakes up until he goes to sleep at night, all my boy does is eat sugar. It makes him crazy and it is bad for his body. Please, tell me what to do."

The swami looked at the mother and said, "Go home and return in three months."

Disappointed and upset, the mother took her son back home. She returned to the swami three months later.

"Oh, Babaji. The situation is getting worse. My son won't go to school or do his prayers. The sugar is making him uncontrollable. Please, tell me what to do."

The swami looked at the mother and said, "Go home and return in two months."

More disappointed and more upset, the mother took her son back home. She returned two months later.

"Oh, Babaji. I fear for my own health now. My boy never sleeps and now I don't sleep either. I am desperate. Please, tell me what to do."

Once again, the swami sends her home instructing her to return in one month.

When the mother and son returned, the mother could hardly speak. "Oh, Babaji. I fear I can't go on. Please, you must tell me what to do."

The swami looked at the mother and said, "Tell your son to stop eating sugar."

The mother screamed. "Why didn't you tell me this the first time I came to see you? Why did I have to suffer through these months?"

The swami smiled and said, "Because first I had to give up sugar."

And that's the messy truth.

ABOUT THE AUTHORS

About Nicki

I'm a story listener and story-teller. People fascinate me and I have a long and interesting career helping people untangle their stories so they are freed up to write new chapters. I've been fortunate to live and work in different places, to immerse myself in different cultures and companies, to learn different languages and ways of seeing the world and to marvel at our collective humanity and zaniness.

My own journey has been rich; loving family member, prolific writer, expert leadership and team coach, decent enough leader, dear friend, irreverent human being. My soul will always come alive for Motown (my home town), great jazz, Alvin Ailey, meditation, being in the water and my most cherished loved ones.

About Gavin

Mostly, I am a teacher. I help others learn about themselves and their impact in the world. I'm an observer: of people, of cultures, of interactions. And I'm a wanderer: across ideas and places. My interests are at the intersections of history, anthropology, sociology and psychology.

I'm an Englishman, but with an American disposition. I'm also a stellar husband and father, apparently. Professionally, I am an expert leadership and team coach. And I have worked with CEOs and senior executives in many industries all around the world.